A True Story of Pain, C

BURNED AND UNBROKEN

To Deanne,

God bless you, all the best!

Eleanor

ELEANOR BECKER

DR. JERRY HORNER, EDITOR

Dedication

To YOLANDIE, NIEL, Heinz, Matt, Wyatt, Wesley and Walter

Contents

Foreword

THE BIBLE IS FILLED with promises of God's mercy, help, and deliverance in times of trouble, and it's easy to accept and believe those promises in the absence of trials. But how is it when the testing time comes, especially in overwhelming proportion that leaves little or no room for hope of deliverance? How can you trust God when you see medical authorities casting sympathetic glances at you, shaking their heads and whispering among themselves, and at the same time, the person you love most is in an agonizing fight with death? To make matters worse, you are all alone in a strange country with thousands of miles separating you from the loving support of family and close friends.

This was the experience of Eleanor Becker, and in this book, she reveals the reality of the statement found in Psalm 34:19, which says, *"Many are the afflictions of the righteous...."* She and her two-year-old daughter witnessed the tragedy that brought her husband to the precipice of death, where he lingered in indescribable suffering for months. During that time, Eleanor was with her husband in the valley of the shadow of death, and she experienced the reality of the rest of Psalm 34:19 (ESV), *"The LORD delivers him out of them all."*

Everyone knows the story told in Daniel 3 about the three young Hebrews in the fiery furnace. They said, *"Our God whom we serve is able to deliver us..."* (v. 17), and that's about as far as most people read. But the three young men went on to say, "But if not, that's all right too. It doesn't make any difference." Anybody can trust God in the light of deliverance, but how is it in the darkness of hopelessness?

Eleanor's story leaves no doubt that for every shadow there must be a light. Christ is the light of the world, and that includes every dark valley; if you keep your face toward the light, the shadow will fall behind you. This book is a testimony to every person experiencing grief that, if you trust God, He will turn every hurt into a hallelujah and every Calvary into an Easter. He will take every tear and change it into a pearl and make it a diadem for you to wear.

Because of its graphic descriptions of suffering, some of which are beyond imagination, this is not an easy book to read. When you do read it, however, your hope in God will reach a higher level and joyful praise will spring from the depths of your soul. You will agree that it is better to be in a dark valley with Jesus than on a sunlit mountain without Him.

– Jerry Horner, B.A., B.D., M.Div., Th.D.

T HIS STORY OF FAITH, hope and love is the story of a young couple whose faith in the Lord is so strong that it creates miracles which are biblical in nature. "Your faith has made you well" is a statement that Jesus made on numerous occasions when healing people who were afflicted with incurable diseases, even unto death (Mark 5:34, 36; 10:52; Luke 17:19; 18:42; etc). Theirs is also a story of hope, which never falters even when entering *"the valley of the shadow of death,"* the patient's condition is deteriorating, and the chance of survival seems hopeless to the doctors.

This book is a story of love so deep and strong that regardless of the pain, suffering and complications, the love of the Lord and the love of the married couple for each other only grows stronger the worse it gets. Finally, along the way, it is a story of miracles large and small— each of which is vital for the next stage of the journey.

In February 1987, my wife and I received a phone call from a friend who was a professor at Regent University to say that a young student couple had recently arrived from South Africa who would appreciate getting to meet us. My wife Tessa called the number he gave us that evening, and they promptly accepted our invitation to join us for Sunday lunch that weekend.

We thoroughly enjoyed meeting Hennie and Eleanor Becker and their two-year-old daughter Yolandie. We learned that Hennie had recently graduated from Bible college in South Africa and was planning to earn a master's degree in Biblical Studies before returning to their ministry in South Africa. They were a very engaging and enthusiastic family, and since Easter was not too far off, we invited them to spend Easter with our family—a suggestion they immediately accepted.

As the family became more settled, the weather warmed, and they made new friends. We saw them less often, especially as they took the opportunity to tour the USA during the summer. Therefore, when my pager went off one September afternoon, I was surprised to hear Eleanor's voice, calling to say that Hennie had been severely burned in a gasoline explosion and was on his way to Santara Norfolk General Hospital by helicopter. "Can you please help?" she asked.

As the pediatric surgeon-in-chief at the Children's Hospital of the Kings Daughters, immediately adjacent to Santara Norfolk General Hospital (NGH), I had no jurisdiction over adult care at NGH, but I did have hospital privileges there, and I did take "pediatric trauma" calls there on a rotation basis. Consequently, I was familiar with the trauma unit. Also during my pediatric surgery fellowship, I spent a considerable amount of time overseeing the very busy, 30-bed burn unit at the Red Cross Children's Hospital in Cape Town.

When Hennie was carried off the helicopter and brought into the trauma unit, he was still conscious. But as the staff removed the sheet that was covering him, his charred skin, which had adhered to the sheet, simply peeled off his body. The synthetic fibers of his clothing had kept the fire going for a longer period of time, and his skin had the look of burned leather or parchment. At a quick glance, I judged him to have sustained an 80-percent fire burn, and my immediate reaction was "Oh, my! He is not going to survive."

During the 1970s and 80s, burn care improved enormously as the metabolic response to burns became better understood; new, non-toxic, antiseptic drugs for long-term application and respirators became available. Until then, anything more than a 20-percent third-degree burn would most likely result in fatality, but slowly that prognosis improved, provided that the hospital kept pace with the advances. Even so, a 50-percent fire burn was probably the upper limit of survival at that time.

Miraculously, not only had Hennie's health insurance taken effect only the day before his accident, but helicopter transportation to the trauma unit had only recently been instituted, and the burn unit was brand-new as well. All of these factors were essential if he stood any chance of survival. Without rapid resuscitation of fluid loss from an 80-percent burn, Hennie would not have survived the first 24 hours.

However, even with a new and up-to-date burn unit at his disposal, the challenges facing him were enormous, as evidenced by two patients who were admitted within a few days of his admission with significantly lesser-extent burns who did not survive.

In this book Eleanor recounts the physical, emotional and psychological battles the couple endured over the ensuing months. Imagine arriving in a foreign country with a two-year-old child, expecting to attend college while earning enough income on the side to pay the bills and then being faced with a catastrophic situation like this. There was only one source. They had only one sure Source to whom they could turn in such a situation—the Lord.

The purpose of this review is not to recount the incredible suffering a person endures when being treated for a large-scale deep burn, but one example will suffice. When Hennie miraculously survived the acute toxic reaction that occurs during the first several days after a serious burn, the surgeons wanted to start grafting as soon as possible since the area available for harvesting skin was very limited and would need to be re-used over and over again. First, the burn team specialists had to get rid of the dead skin. To effect this process, he was loaded into a "whirlpool" every day. All the dressings had to be soaked off his entire body, and when that painful process was completed, the burn technicians would use scrubbing brushes to scrub the raw surface where dead skin was still attached until it bled. Needless to say, the debridement was extremely painful—even though pain medication was administered beforehand.

He asked me one day if I would please come with him to witness this procedure because "they won't scrub me so hard if you are there." I agreed reluctantly and found to my amazement that the more painful the moment, the more Hennie proclaimed, "Praise the Lord!" I could tell from the volume and frequency with which Hennie "praised the Lord" as to how painful a particular area of scrubbing had been. No screaming and no swearing came from his lips—only "Praise to the Lord!" I came away from that appointment with a totally new concept of what faith should look like.

The Hennie and Eleanor Becker story is a love so deep as to be awe-inspiring, and Eleanor lays it all out in this very personal narrative about her relationship with God and with her husband. She details how she managed to maintain faith even when complications developed, and the doctors did not believe Hennie would survive.

The question is: is it possible for someone to survive an 80-percent fire burn and come through the catastrophe emotionally and physically intact without the love and support of the Lord and family? You have most likely seen pictures of people who were unfortunate enough to be badly burned and left disfigured. Well, if you were to meet Hennie today, you would never suspect that he was ever burned or suffered any other complications. From personal experience, I can say that recovery is a miracle. This book tells you how that miracle happened.

– Donald Nuss, MB, ChB; FRCS©, FACS; FAAP

Preface

WHY WRITE A BOOK thirty years after the fact? As the seasons following the accident came and went, so did the feasibility of writing what was becoming an old story—at least that's what I thought. Turned out the story was not old after all; rather, His story for us became all the more relevant as life went on. It made us stronger, wiser, providing evidence of how God brings beauty from ashes—over and over again.

Living unbroken again after life has broken parts of you becomes the challenge for the future. Wounds of past pain carry the seed of future limitations and destruction, so they deserve to be addressed. When nothing in life makes sense, finding encouragement for a day or so is one thing, but staying in faith for the long haul while holding on to the lesson learned in the valley is quite another.

Statistics confirm that 70 percent of people go through at least one traumatic experience in a lifetime; 20 percent never fully recover. At any given time, 13 million people in America alone suffer negative after-effects from life-changing or life-altering trauma. Sadly, I am not convinced that the numbers are any different for Christ followers. To make matters worse, I believe symptoms of the lingering effects of pain such as flashbacks, nightmares, anger, mistrust, fear, negativity, isolation and the like are not always recognized. Even when they are, chemical intervention becomes the norm instead of real heart healing by the power of God through Jesus Christ. Medicine is a godsend, and I thank God for medication, but it is a feeble replacement for a touch from heaven.

This is why I wrote this book: I believe there is hope and help after life disappoints and disaster burns up your dreams. There is a well of healing from which to drink where everyone is welcome and no sorrow is too great. Even if your pain is private, I want to invite you who hurt to step up one more time and see what is beyond the mountain in front of you. There is light in what seems dark, life for what has seemingly died, and hope when everyone else has given up.

We fell, but we got up again. We were broken, but we experienced healing. We faced setbacks, but we kept walking. We felt joy, and we savored the moments. We encountered love, and we embraced it. We received favor, and we saw Jesus.

Reading this book will not do all of this for you; after all, it's just a book. There is no magic formula; it's just our story. However, ours is an account of the supernatural overarching sovereign providence of God that turned our mourning into dancing. He wants to do the same for you. You can dance again too. You can live unbroken again as well. Yes, you can. I believe you can.

Introduction

READING ABOUT THE ISRAELITES and how they came to the Jordan River after their 38-year journey through the desert offers an astonishing analogy for the lives of today's believers. The children of Israel were on a passage to freedom from slavery during which they had experienced many difficulties, as well as many miracles, including the parting of the Red Sea when God supernaturally freed them from their pursuers.

Next to a river is usually a good place to camp, relax and enjoy nature under pleasant circumstances. The Jordan must have been quite a beautiful sight and something to enjoy, since the Israelites had arrived during the season when the river was always in full flood. The Bible states that the Jordan overflowed its banks during the entire season of harvest. Ten to twelve feet of water would rush by at any given time.

This day was different though. Camping or relaxing next to the river was not the destiny of God's people. After all, they were still on the wrong side of the river. The promise that awaited them was on the other side. There were many of them, and they must have been ready to take the Promised Land after so much time in the desert. The day had come for them to cross the river and leave behind the treacherously long trek in the wilderness.

In the midst of the rushing river and their wilderness circumstances, the children of Israel had to step out in faith and walk into the river. Their only other option was to die to their destiny should they set up camp and get comfortable on the wrong side of the river. Taking that option would have meant dying in the desert—never to experience the plan and promises of God.

What is your next step of faith in pursuit of your promise? For me today, this pen represents my feet, and this book represents the river. I am putting pen to paper as a step of faith to initiate part of my life's purpose, as well as that of many other sojourners around me today and in the days to come. May this writing enable you, the reader, to see how God holds back the walls of water for all who will keep moving forward and forsake camping comfortably on the wrong side of the river.

Come, journey with me as I would like to share the beauty of my Jesus, the power of our God and how He saved my husband's life, and how He restored my family. May this book be a reminder for those who read that God's ways are not our ways, but are always higher and less traveled, yet His ways lead to life, destiny, and success. As a matter of fact, God is *the way*. He becomes the way as we place our feet in the river, the pen on the paper, and stand up one more time during hard and confusing times, so giving life to what we really believe about God.

May these words of my mouth and this meditation of my heart
be pleasing in your sight, LORD, my Rock and my Redeemer.
(Psalm 19:14 NIV)

I wish I could write this book about how life is a breeze and how all you have to do is catch the wind and soar. But I cannot. That would be only one side of an incredibly complex reality. Life on earth requires us to be strong, and becoming strong involves pain. Plain and simple. Just enjoying what our minds reason to be happiness will leave us weak and defeated, without an understanding of the immense power of God and never experiencing all God has planned for us. Jesus won the war on the Cross, but we are still called to fight battles here on earth that will enforce goodness in a realm that leaves us vulnerable to defeat.

A true earth-side understanding of the greatness of our Creator requires more than a mere understanding with our minds. When His power works in and through us as followers of Christ, we, in our weakness, come alive to a glimpse of the supernatural power of God and the deep potential inside each one of us to connect with Him personally. When we taste a piece of what was lost in the garden of Eden when God and man ceased to walk together in unity, it is more than life-*changing*; it is *life-finding*.

Life on earth requires pushing, resisting, and pursuing. We all have our different battles to fight that serve as barriers and threaten to hold us back from finding true purpose and goodness in life. Avoiding the battles could leave us living in a defeated godless state, rummaging through obstacles and never getting ahead. How sad! But there is a high plan for all of us—even a perfect plan for our life.

Fighting and aggression are not really in my natural DNA, but hell and high water have caused me to run to the God who trains my hands for battle. Yes, He still is training me. Life offers obstacles, even taunting giants threaten to render us depressed, anxious, and angry. God wants to be our Commander-in-Chief as we engage in the war against our Enemy. Early in my life I learned about the armor of God, including the sword of the Spirit. I envisioned this beautiful, huge, shiny, sharp and sexy sword, but when the fight got real, blood was found all over it. Enemy blood. There are times to sit peacefully and shine our swords, but only to be ready to fight through hell to get to the success God has set aside for those who serve Him. Blood on my sword, blood on my hands, wounded at times, weak and weary in some seasons, but with tenacious fierce faith I continue to fight to win! I oftentimes do not feel like fighting, but I am glad I have God to give me courage to pull myself up by my own bootstraps and take the land!

Sometimes it is one simple step into the river, i.e., the unknown, the scary, or the vulnerable. Sometimes it is a challenging leap right beyond what was perceived as a limitation. Other times it is a bold move or even a bloody fight. We fight when we have to fight, leap when we have to leap, step when we have to step, and sometimes stand when we have to simply stand. Don't let go of God's promises, your dreams and desires. The win is not only for us, but also for others with us—our own children and loved ones, as well as for generations to come!

Praise be to the Lord my Rock, who trains my hands for war, my fingers for battle. (Psalm 144:1 NIV)

God knows what He is doing. Stand up one more time. Step out one more time. Don't look back, but fix your eyes on what is ahead. If your destiny is still beyond the river, let's go! You have all it takes to keep going and see God fight for you as you stay in faith and act like one who is not alone. Giants may be in front of you, but God is beside you. Don't settle. Never settle. God is much too big for you to keep living in pain or regret.

It's not too late.

The time has come.

My Prayer

GOD, IT HURT BACK then; it has also hurt since then, and I know it's going to hurt again. Please help me to get this story out for Your glory. I ask You to hold my heart, for I am weak. I'd rather do something else, something fun for the moment, but I dedicate this time to You.

Use my life, my pain, and my victories to bring hope back to weary hearts filled with questions and disappointment. If I had a choice, I would rather hide all of this and "move on"—just like many readers do. But search our hearts, answer our cries, bring peace, and draw us closer to You.

You are lovely. You are worthy to be celebrated by every breath we take. So do Your will and have Your way!

1

Is This Really Happening?

Facing Realities and Questions When Disaster Strikes

"I'M SORRY, BUT YOU need to prepare yourself for the worst. Your husband may not be alive by the time we get to the hospital," the emergency medical technician warned. No one ever wants to hear those words; nonetheless, they came without warning on that fateful Friday afternoon in September. The EMT's dire warning fell on me like a ton of bricks, and in an instant, our lives and future were forever changed.

The *Nightingale* medical helicopter from Santara Norfolk General Hospital in Norfolk, Virginia, airlifted my husband, Hennie, from the scene of the accident. The police officer briefly questioned me about what happened and then offered to transport me to the ER where I would meet with Hennie and the medical team. Upon arrival at the hospital, I was relieved to see he was still alive, but nothing in this world could have prepared us for what had just happened or what was to follow in the days, weeks, months, and even years to come.

The Burned Body

A body that suffers and survives extensive burns from a fire faces the start of a long restoration process rather than immediate healing following the injury. Serious burn trauma on a human body becomes worse before ever getting better. This is especially true when suffering a loss of eighty percent or more of the body's skin, which provides protection against heat, light, injury, and infection. When the skin, which is the body's largest organ, is decimated by whatever means, the body is propelled into complete shock, leaving it vulnerable, unprotected, raw, and excruciatingly painful. Confusion, swelling, infection, and every kind of evil suddenly seems to have permission to wreak havoc on the victim.

I know of no good way to burn skin off the body, and what made Hennie's situation so devastating and dire was the way in which he was burned. The accident occurred while he was fixing the carburetor on our van. He accidentally spilled gasoline on his bare skin, and it caught fire. The fuel burned and devoured everything it touched with licking flames and in a cloud of thick black smoke. Flames literally covered his body as he jumped out of the van and ran across the street toward some grass where he could drop and roll.

Thank God, I was in a car right behind him, so I was the first person to reach him. As I ran toward him, I screamed, "Take off your clothes!" Then I saw that both his short trousers and shirt were covered in flames. He tried to rip off his burning clothes as he ran toward the grass. I kept screaming as loudly as I could, "Someone! Call 9-1-1!" Thankfully, someone did.

When I got to where he was lying on the grass, I could not believe my eyes. *What just happened?* In those brief moments, my husband and I were instantly plunged into the worst nightmare we could ever imagine. Worse yet, we would find that neither of us would wake up from it any time soon. My helpless and now naked husband had collapsed on the grass; I took off some of my clothes to cover him.

I heard him mumbling something, so I leaned in closer to hear what he was trying to say. He was not talking to me or any other person; instead, he was praying and praising God. Though he was totally traumatized, he fully comprehended he could have died right then and there, but his trusted "go-to" reaction was connecting with his God. He knew he needed God to stay alive and keep breathing.

I thought for sure that the prayers and praise I was hearing in this situation meant that he was looking at the face of God and probably dying. How could I know at the time that I would soon see many similar scenes of my husband's worshipping God in the midst of the unspeakable pain he was yet to suffer as a result of this traumatic injury.

Grace Came

Revisiting the details and telling the story afterward are in some ways worse than going through this horrible nightmare because I was overshadowed with God's grace in a very supernatural way. I find the experience hard to explain. The best way I know how to describe God's grace is the feeling of being covered with a warm blanket on a very chilly night. I remember literally feeling the presence and grace of God settling down on and around me in the police car on the way to the hospital. That unforgettable moment will always be one of my miracles in life. I did not choose what to think and feel at the time, but I knew God had overshadowed me with great grace and comfort. I was keenly aware of God's grace enfolding me.

I remember talking to the police officer in the car on our way to the hospital. I told him that should my husband die that day he was ready to face God. "He will be in heaven, and I have peace in the knowledge that I have loved him the best I know how. I have no regrets." I am not sure where I found the strength to say all that I said, but I now know that my clarity was totally within the grace of God. With God's grace also comes an uncanny boldness, so I started questioning the officer about his life and what if he had been the one who was facing death and eternity.

I wasn't sure what he was thinking about my interrogation, but I didn't care one iota because my husband was dying, and I had nothing more to lose. So I asked, "While we are facing death here, what about you, Mr. Officer? Are you ready to meet God?"

I cannot remember his response—quite possibly there was none. I have prayed for that police officer over the years, and I have trusted

God to deal with his heart in the event he was not ready to meet Him. A bold and fighting spirit came over me during that ride to the hospital; God knew I would need it for what was ahead.

My utter joy that Hennie was still alive upon our arrival at the ER was short-lived. I rushed to him and immediately saw the condition of his body. The once flawless skin on that previously athletic and perfect body looked like it had simply been ripped off, leaving charred skin hanging in shreds and smelling of death. The third-degree burns he had suffered had swallowed up all the layers of his skin and even the muscle tissue in some areas. Other parts of his body had suffered second-degree burns and what was left of his skin was primarily singed and scorched.

Can it get any worse? Yes, death would be worse. What is worse though—dying or living in a hell like this? This feels like death still breathing!

Once again the grace of God kicked in and rescued me from completely falling apart at the sight and revolting smell of my beloved's body. Hennie, on the other hand, was in a place I don't think anyone could describe. According to the doctors, he was dying with little-to-no chance of survival. Suddenly trapped in a severely burned body, he had no way of escape. The torment and agony he was suffering was beyond human comprehension; his whole world had closed in on him. The seconds in every minute he was still alive became shorter as each and every breath he was still able to take grew weaker.

The World Became Dark and Small

The medical personnel scooped him up from where the ambulance dropped him off and responded with the best treatment they could offer. His condition was very grim. The fight for his life began with barely any evidence of breath left in him—evidence that seemed to slip away and grow fainter during every passing minute. How to survive this trauma was a question with no answers in this world—even in the midst of advanced medical science, medicine, and treatment. His survival was even outside the scope of the medical team who cared for him with great skill and devotion.

I left Hennie in the emergency room and made my way upstairs to the waiting room of the Burn Trauma Unit in Santara Norfolk General Hospital. Only a few people, who had obviously been there for a while and were trying to get some sleep, were in the silent, darkened room. Still, it was the only place I wanted to be—except for next to Hennie. I sat in a daze for what felt like an eternity, waiting for someone to come tell me how Hennie was doing. "O God, please let it be good news!" I cried silently. Questions flooded my mind. *What are they doing with him? Is he still alive? Why are they taking so long?*

My world instantly dwindled to having only room for the next update on Hennie's condition and taking care of Yolandie, our two-year-old daughter. I found myself alone in a "foreign land" with this precious little girl and a severely burned husband. *How on God's earth am I going to keep it together and keep breathing? I am not ready to bury my husband and rear our baby alone!* We had no family close by as they were all living in our homeland of South Africa. Everything we knew and everyone who loved us lived on the other side of the globe, which is very far even in the best of times!

I'm Alone, or Am I?

Dr. Jerry Horner served as the Dean of Biblical Studies at CBN University (now Regent University) in Virginia Beach, where Hennie was a student at the time of the accident. We had known him and his family for only nine months at that time. They were the very first family we met when we arrived in the United States from South Africa. Dr. Horner was one of God's divine setups in our lives, and although we no longer live in the same area, our hearts are forever fused and our lives forever benefiting from having shared life with the Horner family.

After the accident, Dr. Horner was one of the first to visit us in the hospital. The love and compassion that shone from this man's life into ours was nothing short of a piece of heaven! His wife Annie had embraced and loved us from the time we met. She is the most gracious, accepting, kind, and loving person you'll ever meet. Her strong faith in God and wisdom in life have guided me many times and still serve as an example for me to emulate. The Horners remained committed to support and love us through this very dark time of our lives and deserve great honor for being so humble and real—always ready to uplift another.

Dr. Horner is a great theologian and one of the greatest teachers of the Word of God of our time. He was speechless at the news of what had happened that day; on his first visit all he could find at the time to comfort us and apply to the situation was one verse—1 Corinthians 10:13, which says that God will never allow us to be tempted above what we can endure. I can vividly recall his encouraging us with that Scripture and assuring us that God had not deserted us, but would walk with us through this horrible ordeal. He was a representative of the nature and heart of God to us, repeatedly telling us that God would not allow us to walk through something He knew we could not bear. We believed him.

Where the Human Mind Goes When in Pain

Did God do this or even allow it? Have we done something wrong? Is God angry at us or cutting us down to size? Was our sin so big that we are being punished so harshly? Does God not love us like He loves others? Is God killing Hennie? If so, why, and why so gruesomely? Had not Jesus taken our punishment for sin, knowing none of us is perfect? Why are preachers talking so much about prosperity, and are those who suffered and bled second-hand citizens of heaven? Are we even going to heaven? Is this all a bad joke—to believe God is good, while, in reality, He is angry and upset at us? We could probably never please God or be good enough, so why even try? Give up on God and die. This heaven stuff is for others and not us.

These are the thoughts that find permission to land in broken hearts, but they are very far from the truth. These thoughts come easily and naturally to our minds. What we do with these questions is crucial for the quality and outcome of our lives. While it is not wrong to ask questions, not all of them have answers that will completely satisfy. Some may never be answered. You may not like some answers; God will clarify others in time. The renewal of our minds is crucial for spiritual, godly living. So what then is the truth about suffering and this Scripture?

A Deeper Understanding

At the time of the accident and throughout Hennie's subsequent recovery, I thank God that these negative, evil thoughts were not at all in the forefront of my mind. Ours was a fight of life or death each moment, so I simply had no energy to try to figure out things. I had to stay in faith, stand up, show up, shape up, look up, and fight while there was still breath. I was not in the least concerned about the God questions in other people's hearts; somehow I knew I had to focus and resist death in order to see life. A marvelous power works in a weak vessel that totally trusts in God. Marvelous!

As a matter of fact, the aftermath of the whole ordeal of suffering and restoration is where my deepest struggles started. I will address more about that battle in a later chapter. Long after the actual situation was over, the memories lived on with a vengeance in my mind and heart. The after-effects of deep trauma have the power to ruin a lifetime of what God has called healed and restored, and that is a fight in and of itself.

I believed God's Word with all of my heart, yet, simultaneously, I knew this life interruption was so far above what I could ever bear.

Words cannot begin to explain how desperately I was clinging to 1 Corinthians 10:13 throughout the battle, and the Scripture would remain my guiding light for months to come. A picture literally formed in my mind of clenching a rope in the middle of a vicious dark storm while dangling over certain death. A deeper understanding of this verse grew in my heart as time passed, bringing light to my life that helped me understand something more about the nature and character of God.

> *No temptation has overtaken you except such as is common to man; but God is faithful, who will not allow you to be tempted beyond what you are able, but with the temptation will also make the way of escape, that you may be able to bear it.*
>
> (1 Corinthians 10:13)

The two of us were in the very claws of death—Hennie literally and I in every other sense. Ours was definitely within the realm of something we could not humanly bear. *Where is God? What about this Scripture?* The revelation to me was that the Bible does not say that we will never go through something we cannot bear but that we will never be tempted above what we can endure. What is the difference? The pain and trial is not the temptation because trauma and pain do kill many dear followers of Christ, and all of us will eventually die.

I discovered that the temptation is what comes in the midst of the painful situations, and we must choose how to respond to it. We either curse God, which leads to sin and death, or endure temptation by clinging to God, which leads to approval and the crown of life. Temptation draws us to blame someone, give up, lash out, hit back, or resort to the many other fleshly responses and retaliations in times of trouble.

The source of temptation is never God because God does not tempt anyone. In our trials, our temptations come from our flesh and Satan.

1 Peter 4:12 says the fiery trial tempts us. Galatians 4:14 asserts that the temptation comes from the flesh. Luke 4:13 clearly states the source of temptation is the Devil! The book of James says to let no man say God tempts him.

The word *temptation* used in these instances means "to test maliciously or inflict evil to prove character and faith." This meaning clearly is not in character for God. The truth is bad and painful events happen on this earth, and in that respect, we are tempted to react in destructive ways. But God provides a way out for us! I thought and knew for sure that neither Hennie nor I would be able to endure this pain. Yet we were able to resist the plethora of temptations that came as a result of the trial and keep on staying in faith that God loved us and was fighting for and with us.

We are still resisting temptations that come through pain and disappointment, and as long as we are alive, we will have to face and resist the temptation to react in fleshly and ungodly ways, especially during painful events or circumstances.

Blessed is the man who endures temptation; for when he has been approved, he will receive the crown of life which the Lord has promised to those who love Him. Let no one say when he is tempted, "I am tempted by God"; for God cannot be tempted by evil, nor does He Himself tempt anyone. But each one is tempted when he is drawn away by his own desires and enticed. Then, when desire has conceived, it gives birth to sin; and sin, when it is full-grown, brings forth death. Do not be deceived, my beloved brethren. Every good gift and every perfect gift is from above, and comes down from the Father of lights, with whom there is no variation or shadow of turning. (James 1:12-17)

Endurance is abiding in the faith that God's Word is true and that He loves you and will never leave you. In enduring, He gives you the way out of the temptation to sin and brings you into His marvelous grace and power. With God, every temptation to follow the flesh and become bitter also has a way out to overcome and to grow. For Hennie and me, the choice was between life and death. We had no other way but to endure and allow God to lead us along the path out of this ordeal. We chose God and held on to this promise—that was about all we were able to do.

Who Can Help?

I'll never forget how helpless I was and how deep in the claws of death Hennie was. His broken body even smelled like death. Every night when I went home, I would take one last look at him, not knowing if I would ever see him alive again. Some nights I'd get as far as the door to his room and stop, stare back at him and cry one more silent prayer to God. Those moments are frozen in time, accompanied by the smell of the chemicals, bandages and even the mask and robe I had to wear while in his room.

The doctors could not give us much hope for a good outcome. They dressed the wounds and treated the body all the while knowing full well that my husband's healing was not in their hands, but in a far more supernatural process. There seemed to be no safe place on earth to hide. All we could see in this physical world was a young, godly husband and father trapped in a burned-up, bandaged-up, and messed-up body! *How could this be?*

It was not the time to start asking God questions; rather, we needed to focus on fighting, resisting doubt, believing what I knew to be true about God and draw strength from the One who lived inside of me. We needed power and healing from heaven! We needed a miracle and grace to keep going. We needed not to faint nor grow weary but to stay in unwavering faith in the One who was able to do exceedingly abundantly above and beyond what our feeble minds could comprehend. I thank God that we were not alone and for the body of Christ who stood with us in prayer and faith when we were in the throes of death and weakness.

In the midst of my unwavering faith in God, though, I was still very weak and found myself unable at times even to quote Scripture. I knew and believed it in my heart, but I was too exhausted during those early days to recite it. I believe verses were echoing in my heart all the time, although my usual prayer times with God were now different.

I was so strong but suddenly so weak. Being able to quote Scripture by book and verse suddenly didn't matter to me anymore. I needed more than knowledge and information; I was facing a crisis of belief that went deeper than biblical knowledge alone. Knowing and believing became two separate matters to me. I didn't simply know the Scripture; I relied on it to give us power to resist the darkness and death that were at our door. I believed the Word of God was at work even when I couldn't pray. We were experiencing a time of going beyond the mind and believing past the natural that every promise in God's Word was active, alive and being fulfilled in our situation.

God Will Do This for You!

Something beautiful happens when God takes over where our feeble efforts can no longer make a difference. When the trauma hit, the Word of God in our hearts stood up and became more real than the physical drama that engulfed us, becoming our very life and enabling us to continue breathing and seeing the face of Jesus amid the pain and despair.

In good times, eat the Word, drink it, and live it so that when you are in dire need, it will ooze from your spirit to keep and comfort you in great power! During those first weeks, all I could do at times was pick up the Bible and simply hold it close to my heart. I was broken and exhausted. I often slept with its pages open next to me. I felt almost paralyzed, yet found my way to the book of Psalms to read out loud. Any psalm, any verse—it was all God's Word and hearing the sound of it was all good. I needed hope and life—not judgment, reasoning, or even deep theology. In my weakness, God was strong in me, and I'll forever be grateful for this miracle.

Needing to Understand It All

Students of the Bible and well-intentioned people questioned me throughout this trial about the reason all of this might have been happening and how it could possibly have been prevented. One such question was, "If you had stayed in South Africa, would this incident have happened?" I trusted this was a well-meaning question, but the inquiry was accompanied by a very sharp sword that had the potential to cut my heart right out of my chest!

That particular question reminded me of and felt like the sleek old snake asking those questions that are designed essentially to sow doubt about the power and love of God in our life. What were those questions insinuating? Were we being reprimanded for following what we deeply believed was the will of God for our lives? Should we have ignored the call we heard from God to study in the USA? Or was the question coming from someone who needed answers to life's difficult questions—often impossible to answer?

"Where is God in all of this heartbreak?" sounds like a good question coming from a fellow student of theology. First of all, when someone is in the claws of death or grief, don't ask these kinds of questions. In fact, don't voice any questions; instead, shine the light of Jesus. Striving to answer those questions is walking where angels fear to tread—even when times are good. Everyone tries to avoid pain, but to think by understanding everything we will have peace and joy, and never go through tough times, is far from the truth.

This thinking may make sense if you haven't lived long enough.

At some point, however, life will offer you questions that will not be answered this side of heaven. What will you do with those? This is one of life's most difficult mountains to climb. Why would such an atrocity happen to someone who professes to have followed God to a land far away, leaving the motherland, family, and familiar surroundings after hearing clearly from God. Did God lead you to come halfway around the world to be burned up and die? Well, no. Then it must be that you are fools to have thought you heard from God because it could not have been God.

The body of Christ was our safe place, and I never knew the level of love and support we received existed. Even so, some people had deep questions when they saw such sadness and unthinkable pain. Some voiced those questions, and some probably secretly wondered. If it had been up to the real spiritual interrogators, we were doomed—burned up, dying, and outside the will of God. I've often wondered if the spiritual philosophers with their deep theological discernment feel accomplished and satisfied in finding answers to life's tough questions. Well, that is, until tragedy strikes them.

Yes, allow me to be a little cynical briefly since someone may read and realize God is bigger than our lives and knowledge, and His Word is true in all circumstances. Blaming human weakness as an excuse for what we sometimes see as abandonment by God (as if God abandons us simply because we are weak creatures) is so easy. God loves us, He never leaves us, and neither does He punish us for our foolishness. If that assumption were true, we'd all be dead now!

I do believe that we can find ourselves in harm's way because of foolish decisions, sin, and disobedience. Then there is Job, a righteous man who suffered greatly before God restored and multiplied back to him what he had lost. So after all we've been through and according to God's Word, we are to stay in faith, encourage one another, never doubt God's love for us, and never judge harshly for the sake of condemning someone.

I have read many books about the question of where God is when Christians suffer. While some are truly comforting, God is the only One to interpret the answer fully, which will be completely understood when we look into His glorious face.

Let's Figure It Out

The true tragedy is thinking you always have or must have God and life figured out. That mindset may work for you and make you feel good for a while, but only until those calculations don't add up anymore. This superiority will only last until you have to face the unexplainable in your own life. Sadly, that is the reason and the time when many followers of Jesus Christ turn away in despair and defeat, blaming God for what happened. How unfortunate! We have all seen this scenario far too many times: believers who once were on fire for God but lost their way in the clouds of trials and temptations.

Many of life's deepest questions will only be answered on the other side of eternity. As followers of Christ, we should accept that truth. This life is simply too corrupted to attempt to understand it all, and for that reason, we are called to a life of faith. If we had all the answers, faith would not be necessary. What never changes is that God is good—all the time.

Bad things do happen to good people! Jesus said He came to bring a sword, so there is a war. There is tension in this life and because you walk in the kingdom of God and are spiritual does not exclude you from the sadness this world contains. If that were the case, we would not need grace, which is ours exactly for this reason: to walk in the power of God no matter what we go through and believe that, with God, the best is always yet to come. Our lives are witnesses of how God can take death and deep despair, and restore it to beauty and great joy!

How About You?

Maybe you have fears that torment you or pain in some area of your life for which you have no answers or understanding. These are a very real threat to your salvation and relationship with God. Just picking someone—even God—to blame when you are hurting and walking away is convenient. You can walk away from God and His ways and plans, but be assured you will take with you all your hurt and pain. Eventually, that hurt will manifest in your life in the form of broken relationships, anger, constant disappointment, and unfulfilled expectations.

Don't allow that to take place. Don't look for answers; rather, look into the face of Jesus. He suffered greatly and understands what you are going through. This life is not all there is, but only a fraction and a breath in time—compared to life eternal. The Bible says that death is the final enemy. It is a door we have not experienced, but God is on the other side of it. Lay down those heavy questions in the presence of God and take up a new position of faith and closeness to God, who is the answer. He wants you tight with Him where hope and healing is in your future.

2

Beautiful People

Trusting People You Love When Tragedy Strikes

THE WAITING ROOM IN the burn trauma unit of the hospital where Hennie was treated became much more familiar to me in the months following the accident than I would have ever wanted. When I first saw him in the emergency room after the Nightingale helicopter transported him to the hospital, I told him that everything was going to be fine now that he was safely in the care of a very skilled medical team. I begged him to hold on and take courage for he would soon feel better once they started to take care of the wounds he had sustained.

He lay in the ER, wrapped up and helpless like an injured animal. Only God knew what was lurking under those hospital blankets that covered his severely burned body. I also told him that I had overheard that he was going to be bathed and cleaned up. I felt surely that kind of care would soothe his pain and make him completely comfortable. I truly thought he would feel better at the time, yet Hennie was about to experience quite the opposite from the reality I had expected.

Desperate for Some Good News

I was desperate to help him with some positive news and aid him in his recovery from this horrible accident. Finding some way to help him was all I could think about during those first several hours. In my mind, he had survived the accident, and no matter how horrible and extensive his injuries were, he was over the worst; everything was about to get better soon. Little did I know about the fierce battle ahead and the time and torture he would endure before anything would get any better. The baths we thought were going to soothe the pain were only the beginning of a very dreadful road ahead to be experienced as nothing short of a torture chamber.

The first line of treatment that day was the wound cleaning in the form of scrub baths. Technicians specifically trained to care for burn victims laid his raw body on a stretcher and lowered it into a tub of Clorox water where they scrubbed—yes, scrubbed—the dead skin off his body. Once I learned the truth about the baths, I could only think that although the flames hadn't killed him, this process might very well push him over the edge.

Raw flesh and nerves were exposed to elements they were never meant to survive, but the dead cells on and around all the burn wounds were the most imminent threat to his survival. These dead cells needed to be removed several times a day, as his naked soaking body and exposed nerves were mercilessly scrubbed with a hard sponge. Dead cells could cause and host infection, providing free breeding ground for bacteria to invade and destroy what was left of his skin as well as the deeper tissues of the body. If any infection were to get into this one huge open wound covering 80 percent of his body, death would have been certain.

After the wounds were scrubbed in the tub for the first time, a true assessment was made as to the real damage to my husband's body. The findings were that the burns were severe and worse than initially thought. But thank God, he was still alive! I could never explain how I always expected to hear good news during Hennie's hospitalization. I didn't begin to understand the cloud of grace that surrounded me with the strength I needed to expect something good to happen any minute of every day. I was in a constant state of expecting good news, waiting for someone to break the news to me that Hennie's condition was not as bad as it seemed. But that word never happened. Yet, in the months to follow, I had a supernatural buffer to all the bad news I kept hearing. Just as well, because bad news was the news of the day—every day.

The Valley of Torture

What the nurse called *hymns* were worship songs (I guess she only knew about hymns), and it was very clear to all the staff in that room that he was worshipping God during the procedure. *He's singing spiritual songs in the scrub tub? He is praising God while the raw wounds are being scrubbed? That's good,* I thought. If he is singing and praising God, it must be an indication that all is well. As it turned out, those were songs of worship and adoration to God in order to survive the pain and torture that pushed him to the absolute edge of death.

The scrubbings became standard daily treatment in a world where there was no night. The burn unit never sleeps, the lights never go out, and the days are 24 hours long. There is no sleep or slumber in the world of severely burned patients, rather, around-the-clock treatment, assessment, and care.

Hennie told me afterward that the pain was so intense he knew he would have died the moment he gave up the fight to live. The power to stop breathing was in his hands, and he could have literally stopped living at any time if he had chosen to do so. He came chillingly close but never crossed that line of giving up his will to live. He has a phenomenal testimony of how praising God in the midst of the worst pain saved his life. His ordeal was unspeakable. Death was literally dangling over him. Even in the smell of the burned flesh that remained on him for a long time, death made itself known and was very near. It felt as if death was guarding him and ready to pounce the very moment it could swallow its prey. Horrible.

Hospitals are places of healing where incredibly skilled people save lives and dress wounds, but they are also where death is most active and concentrated. Evil pounces on the weak, so in that sense, I came to believe a hospital is probably the worst place for a very sick person to be.

Thank God for God-fearing doctors and nurses and faith-filled friends and family! The Word of God states that our days were numbered in heaven before we ever lived any, so we kept believing that despite the evil and death surrounding Hennie, he was going to live the number of days in God's mind and no less. His battle was not easy, but we fought to stay in faith and see him healed and restored. Some day.

> *In Your book they all were written, the days fashioned for me, when as yet there were none of them.* (Psalm 139:16)

My First Visit

I was finally allowed to see Hennie after his first scrubbing session. I remember walking into the room to the bed where he was lying, and my first impulse was to touch and comfort him. I looked at his body and could not find a spot to touch or hold him where it wouldn't hurt. It seemed like his body was bandaged, salved, gauzed and raw everywhere. It was not the body I knew that morning before I left the house, but one now tormented and destroyed by the devastating effects of flames burning a human body. He was wrapped up in bandages and held in position with slings and contraptions with which I was unfamiliar. He was unrecognizable.

As I walked closer to him, I didn't recognize his face as it was swollen to twice its size. I did recognize his eyes, though, as he looked at me from a body that seemed ready to separate from his soul at any instant. His fingertips were sticking out from the bandages on his arms that were elevated in slings to prevent swelling as much as possible.

I desperately looked for a part of his body that was recognizable—somewhere I could touch. His toes, I recognized his toes, and they had skin on them so I gently touched them. From there, it was raw flesh and lots of bandages everywhere. Strange as it may seem, my brain has taken a snapshot of that moment when I stared at his toes. This was my husband for real. Those were my husband's toes that looked so beautiful and unaffected by the flames. The rest of his body, not so much. I was staring in disbelief, and reality had no room in my mind at that time. What I saw simply did not fit into my framework of understanding.

His face had been singed from the licking flames of his burning clothes, and he smelled like burned flesh. The repulsive smell of burning hair and skin hung heavily around his body. The bottom of his chin as well as his nose and his eyebrows were scorched. Tips of his hair near his face were singed. His head of black hair was all intact, and those loving eyes became begging eyes that day and for the weeks to follow. It was as if he begged me to take him home, get him out of there and make it all go away.

The physicians had explained that they were doing whatever they could to help control the pain without totally sedating him. The doctors feared that if they were to sedate him, he would die. Hennie was awake all of the time, as he was purposely kept in a waking state so he could fight to stay alive. The staff and technicians were constantly talking to him while they treated him to keep track of his responsiveness and state of consciousness.

When I was finally allowed to be in the room during many of the procedures, they encouraged me to talk to him and keep him engaged and awake. It would have been better for Hennie to "sleep" through all that time, but it was not to be. Staying alive required an effort on his part—no matter how badly he was injured or how close to death he came. What a fighter he was!

Faith-Filled Young Dreamers

We were young, filled with dreams and plans for the future. Thank God we were young and healthy. Hennie's 28-year-old athletic body was in perfect physical shape. He had a very strong body and had never smoked, which became very important in his fight for survival after the burns.

We had arrived from South Africa, only nine months prior to the accident, to live in Virginia Beach, where Hennie worked on his master's degree in theology. We—Hennie, our two-year-old daughter Yolandie, four suitcases, and I—had embarked on this amazing adventure upon boarding an Air France flight from Johannesburg to New York.

Seriously, everything the three of us started life with in the USA was contained in those four suitcases. The lack of earthly stuff was well compensated for by the abundance of courage and zeal to go for our dreams and live a successful and God-fearing life.

Hennie had graduated from the AFM Bible Seminary in Johannesburg just months prior to our departure for the United States. Toward the end of his seminary studies, we fasted and prayed to hear from God where His will was for us to pastor a local church in South Africa. After all, pastoring was the next logical step after completing his studies, and we had three possible locations to consider. We wanted to hear from God where to go. After some time, we both felt the leading of God to move temporarily to the United States for Hennie to work on his postgraduate studies at CBN University.

For us South African kids to be part of such a great Christian university was an opportunity of a lifetime. We prepared to take this step of faith into a pioneering and exciting experience. We knew without a shadow of doubt that we had heard from God and He was with us; we were all in.

New Country, Different Culture

America was completely unfamiliar to us; after all, we had never visited or known anyone from this country. Our plan was to move to Virginia Beach for four years where Hennie planned to obtain his master's degree and unique experience for ministry. This was not an easy decision—not for us nor for our families who did not understand why we wanted to be so extreme. They vowed to pray for us and supported our dreams as they eagerly awaited our return to South Africa where we were going to pastor a local church and live happily ever after.

My mother-in-law once told me that when you are sold out for God and follow His leading, you always know where you start but never where you'll end up. Her words were certainly prophetic and have certainly proven true in our lives—more so than what she would have wanted them to be.

Dr. Jerry Horner was instrumental in helping us to get set up in our own apartment in Virginia Beach. He made arrangements for us to spend our first night with another student, Peter Stepan. Little did we know that Peter would become significant in our destiny twenty years later as one person in a chain of connections that led us to serve as pastors at The Rock Church and World Outreach Center in San Bernardino for twelve years. That God all along had a plan became crystal clear in hindsight a lifetime later.

Dr. Horner also introduced us to "Operation Blessing," a ministry of the 700 Club that helped people in need of items such as furniture, food, etc., and offered us some necessities to get our lives started as international students.

I remember the day Dr. Horner took us to the Operation Blessing warehouse where we found great items like a floral, orange velvet sleeper couch, a wooden bench with plastic upholstered seats, a couple of mismatched chairs, and lamps. How remarkable that the dean of the School of Divinity would take time out of his busy schedule to drive us kids to get furniture from the ministry warehouse. He showed such humility and support that we had never before experienced in our lives. The Horners' garage also held some treasures we were able to use, including beds, side tables and dressers that added to our little collection of needed items.

One day our doorbell rang, and Dr. Horner was behind a big, bulky television he carried into our apartment. Another snapshot was taken in time! He told us that every house in the United States should have a television, and he wanted to see that ours did too. We will never forget this highly educated theologian who was so gifted in teaching the greatness of the kingdom of God, yet he was humble enough to care about a television for our home. Remarkable? Yes!

What in the World?

Halloween came shortly after Hennie's accident, and I didn't know the first thing about what that meant. As I walked into his hospital room the week following the accident, black spider stickers and gross images of death and darkness, hanging from the ceiling and ledges, met me. Fake spider webs were fastened to the doors and windows— even fake witches, skulls and gravestones. Can you imagine my perplexity with what was going on? *What in the world is happening? Is this a bad joke or have some people lost their minds?*

One of Hennie's fellow students came to visit later that day and discreetly removed all of the horrible paraphernalia in and around his room. Then I was really confused! He proceeded to briefly explain the tradition and celebration of Halloween, but for the life of me, I could not grasp the concept at all at the time. I thought that celebrating Halloween was far too complicated for me to understand and decided to deal with the tradition at another time. Not until the following year in October did I really learn what Halloween was all about.

Facing the culture shock had been expected, but not quite like this!

I was stunned by how a whole society could transform their world instantly into a celebration of death everywhere I looked. My husband was dying, so my modus operandi was to pay no attention to it—not even to try to understand it. I ignored it, and eventually it did go away—until October the next year.

God-People

Words cannot explain the absolute treasure God-people are in your life at a time of intense trial. Dr. Don Nuss and his wife Tessa were exactly that to us. They are South Africans who had lived in the USA for fifteen years at the time we met in Norfolk, Virginia. Shortly after our arrival in America, Tessa heard about us from a friend and invited us to join them for the upcoming Easter. We had a wonderful time at their home and enjoyed the most delicious roasted lamb this side of the Atlantic. This memorable Easter celebration sealed our friendship forever with this wonderful and godly family.

Our American Easter traditions were established with the Nuss family for all the years we lived on the East Coast. Even now, while our grown kids enjoy mostly vegan lifestyles in California, we think of the Nuss family every Easter when everyone partakes of delicious roasted lamb. The kids refrain from eating meat, so for Easter I cook them lamb—our family's favorite line from *My Big Fat Greek Wedding*.

Tessa taught me so many things, especially life things. She truly loves people, which is evidenced in how much joy she finds in entertaining, cooking, and caring for friends and others. And she can cook! Not too shabby for an English girl to cook such tasty South African food. The Afrikaners sometimes find English cooking bland, but Tessa has destroyed that theory. Seasoning is serious stuff for South African foodies, which most of us are. She is no exception, and to prove her ability, she also made the best carrot cake in the whole wide world. She never would share her secret recipe though—not even with me. As I said, food is serious business to us. When Yolandie got married, she received the recipe as a wedding gift. Tessa's carrot cake recipe has now become a Becker secret also.

Tessa could whip up a roast chicken and veggies in no time, and only Don could carve that bird so perfectly. I'll miss those beautiful times forever, with Yolandie running up and down the curved staircase in their home along with the three Nuss girls. I will forever miss those interesting and inspiring visits at the fireplace in the winter. All four girls, by the grace and goodness of God, are grown now and have become amazing and very accomplished women. We did well, Tess!

Tessa was the first one in the waiting room the day of the accident and brought me leftovers to eat I'll never forget. Like any good South African mom, she knew I'd get hungry at some point and also knew McDonalds wouldn't do. She also just loves to give, and that day she gave me her presence and leftover chicken. It was perfect and exactly what I needed.

Dr. Nuss worked as a pediatric surgeon at the children's hospital right next to the hospital where Hennie was being treated. Like any loving family member would, they let us stay in their guest room until we could figure out how events would develop over the days that followed. They "adopted" Yolandie for the first two months after the accident, until Hennie's mom arrived from South Africa. This very busy family with tight schedules of school, projects, sports, ballet, and building a successful medical practice, now had a little two-year-old trailing behind Tessa everywhere she went! Yolandie became a part of all the action—her favorite part by far was watching the Nuss girls dance as they prepared for their roles in the annual Nutcracker performance. She was in heaven to see them dance. She fell in love with ballet and spent many of her toddler days in pink tutus as she imitated roles in Swan Lake and the like. Her attempts were more adorable than imaginable.

I was with Hennie from dawn to dusk, sometimes even earlier and later. Yolandie's little two-year-old life was also abruptly interrupted by her dad's accident but forever changed for the good by this experience with the Nuss family. They showered her with attention and care and forever ingrained in her a love for medicine—and ballet, of course!

My Perfect Place

I remember coming home, mostly late at night the first several days after the accident, with all of my concern directed to Hennie's well-being. I soon realized giving Yolandie the attention she deserved was still important, so I tried to be home early enough to put her to bed. Some nights after she had fallen asleep, I'd leave just to go see if Hennie was as comfortable as possible for the night. Yolandie was well cared for, but she missed me; besides, Tessa still had a busy household to run.

Many nights after getting back from the hospital, I determined to put her to bed like we used to do before the accident. She has always loved books, lots of books, and could never get enough of all kinds of bedtime stories and conversations. However, I found myself reading those stories with earnest effort, mostly being unable to follow or comprehend anything about them. The thought of Hennie being alone in the hospital on the brink of death encompassed all my mental capacities. Nonetheless, my day was never complete without holding and loving that little girl as if nothing was wrong. She was my perfect place in a very disrupted world.

Imagining our baby growing up without her daddy was painful to consider, so that thought gave me even more zeal to fight and pray without ceasing for Hennie's recovery. My husband was also the love of my life, and in a million years, I could have never imagined life without him. It was so close, I saw him slip away, I saw him deeply trapped in the claws of death, but thank God, I also witnessed his long road to recovery.

It Was Friday

Then there was the visit from the priest on that fateful Friday afternoon. He was from the Nuss' church, a godsend that I would never forget. He knelt in front of me in that dimly lit waiting room and prayed with great compassion and faith for Hennie's recovery. He left me with the words, "It's Friday (which it was), but Sunday is coming." What a poignant saying that had a much deeper meaning and became a lifeline to me that day! It was also a prophecy that would eventually come true. Sunday for Hennie was not two days away, though, it was more like two years. But it came, and we are grateful!

Dr. Horner, Tessa and the priest were with me that afternoon when our pastor, Jim Kilpatrick, arrived after he heard the news. What a man he was, what a family they were to us, and what a God place for us to have been in that small but powerful church family at the time of the accident! Pastor Jim hugged me, and I broke down. "Can we just leave the hospital so life can go on?" was what I really wanted to ask him. "Could Hennie go back to class, and we attend church on Sunday like we always did?" But all that had changed in an instant. Life as we knew it changed forever that Friday at noon.

I am eternally grateful for Pastor Jim and his wife Judy who, together with the whole church family, supported and loved us without boundaries. Pastor Jim did not miss one single day, but visited us every day during the full duration of Hennie's hospitalization. Anything could have gone wrong on any given day, but we could always count on the certainty of Pastor Jim's visit. Every day he would lay hands on Hennie and pray. He would get the latest update on Hennie's condition and relay it to the prayer teams, so the congregation would pray. They prayed for us, offered practical help, visited us and showered us with gifts and cards. He encouraged us daily to keep fighting and assured us we were not alone. Such commitment was not written in any book on pastoring. In fact, the opposite is probably taught, yet he was that pastor to us—our God-sent pastor and church for that season, and we were grateful!

Love in Action

These people were our family—even closer than family. Before Dr. Horner left the waiting room that day, he asked for my checkbook and the contact information of our landlord. He took over the management of our finances and the paying of our bills, and he made sure many of our practical needs were being met. The lawn got mowed, our house was cleaned, and even our refrigerator was stocked with all kinds of food and ready-to-eat meals. I never had to give a thought to those practical day-to-day responsibilities and was encouraged to focus on Hennie's well-being and medical care.

People near and far supported us during this time of disaster: some brought us cooked meals, many gave money, and others fasted and prayed for Hennie's healing. So many people took action to help us in every way possible—those we knew well and with whom we lived life, as well as countless people from all over the country and world who had heard what had happened. Americans rallied around this young family from Africa and touched our hearts forever!

Never have I known such love and support, and no wonder we were placed on a path to eventually be proud to be called American citizens! Ma Leen, Hennie's mother, said, "The blood transfusions during Hennie's hospitalization put the DNA for American citizenship in his blood." It's quite possible that she might have really believed that to be totally true! Maybe she knew something we didn't, which oftentimes was the case.

On the day of the accident, Yolandie and I spent the night at the Horners' home. Dr. Jerry took the responsibility to contact our family in South Africa with the news about what had happened. Making the call to Hennie's mother back in the homeland was not easy. In fact, all of our family was in South Africa. The news was a shock to everyone and left them helpless in many ways since they were almost 10,000 miles away. We were the crazy-for-Jesus kids who had left on a quest of following God—no matter where He led us. I can't imagine a mother getting that call. Hennie was the baby in his family, and in the eyes of his four siblings, he was his mom's favorite child. She loved each one of them, but he held a special place in her heart. Oh, how she loved him!

Mother and Son

She told me the story that I believe to be the reason for the strong bond between her and her Hennie. He was only eleven days old when his dad died in a mining accident in South Africa. His death, of course, left her totally overwhelmed with five young children to rear without their father. Her little baby became her comfort during a very tragic time in her life. She didn't want to see or talk to anyone, but spent all her days holding and focusing her attention on her newborn son. She found comfort in holding him close to her heart in those times of such deep grief, wondering how she was ever going to make it alone.

She was not your average woman, but brave, smart and hardworking—someone who knew how to make things happen. She could rule a small country. Can't blame her for not trying either. She had the tendency to make things happen in her world—in her own home as well as anywhere she thought help was needed!

I loved my mother-in-law like she was my own mother, which she truly became. She taught me so many crucial life lessons that would need an entire book to contain them. She was heartbroken after hearing the horrible news about Hennie, and without hesitation, this 63-year-old booked a seat on her first transatlantic flight to come see her son and help in any way she could. As a matter of fact, it was her first flight anywhere ever! The things kids can make parents do!

There was a comfort in Ma Leen's presence that was unexplainable.

I knew when she was around that everything was going to be fine—much like my own mother. These were two women of great skill and capacity who had created a world around them of order, comfort, and faith. Ma Leen was the matriarch of her family, and by God's grace, she managed to rear all of her kids through the difficult times of being a single mom and of surviving a failed marriage to "Mr. Tall Dark and Handsome." She was a hopeless romantic deep in her heart, and, yes, she fell for the wrong guy at one point in her life. She then married Edward, the Englishman, who took great care of her even though he didn't seem to have much patience with the kids. But he loved and adored her, which was quite something coming from a rather staunch and serious person. He was a good man.

Oupa Eddie, as he was called, got radically saved after they met, and he became the most saved person in the whole family—almost too saved, if that were possible. He loved God uncompromisingly, was a devoted follower of Christ and a trusted husband. He was also a real gentleman, yet very stubborn at times.

As an older man, he suddenly became very ill, but his medical problems were, of course, much too personal to have doctors prod, poke, and treat him. He remained a dignified English gentleman who went to be with the Lord after this fairly short illness. That's the way he wanted it, and we respected his wishes.

Ma Leen was also the "doctor" in the family. Yolandie was born with those genes, I guess, and she resembles her Grandma Leen in so many ways. I found out very early that, first of all, no mother has loved a son like Ma Leen loved Hennie (prior to my having my own sons, of course), and that, secondly, you should never complain of any ailment whatsoever if you were not willing to take the medicine she would whip up for you. Yes, I mean literally whip up—a little of this, a couple of drops of that, and you'll get well soon. Even if her concoction caused a violent vomiting session, it must have been exactly what you needed to get well. Anybody will feel better after swallowing all that is what I say! The taste of her blend was much worse than the ailment, so it worked for the most part. If not the drops and syrups, the castor oil was a great last resort that improved anyone's health! She was a trip and a treat, and I'm so very honored and fortunate to have had a second mother like her.

She was wonderful in every stubborn and godly inch of her being! Like mother, like son. The Becker stubbornness came to beneficial use in Hennie's fight for his life!

3

The Wounds

Letting Deep Wounds Lead to Deep Healing

May this be a letter by Christ through me,
written not with ink but by the Spirit of the living God,
not on pages of paper, but on pages of flesh,
that is, on the heart of you, reader!

HENNIE'S ACCIDENT HAPPENED BEFORE the days of cell phones with cameras, so I have no pictures to document this time period nor of the haunting memories it left behind. Taking pictures was the furthest thing from my mind. I have often wondered what it would have been like had I taken some. Intense relief that I don't have any pictures immediately follows that thought, as I don't think I could stand to look at what happened again, it would be torture. It may take thousands of words within this book to paint the pictures that bring to life what almost killed my husband, our dreams, and our hopes.

This Is for You, the Reader

More than anything, I desire to create a picture of the devastation in order to contrast it with the amazing grace and power of God through Jesus Christ. I have no emotional strength to go back to relive the nightmare, but in obedience to God's commission to share the miracles that followed, I do. Ours was not an overnight miracle but one that happened over time, and required staying in faith for the long haul. We were plunged into a world of impossibility, unbearable pain, and the temptation to simply give up—a world where it would surely take a miracle to survive. I thank God that He lives in the realm of the impossible and miraculous. That is where God shines brightly—where He manifests His mighty power, meets a broken, weary soul, and works all things together for good—even if it takes time.

I really don't want go back there, but if you will come with me, it is worth the pain. No mountain is too high or valley too low for God. He is always present. His arm is not too short, His ear too dull nor His hand too weak to sustain you in times of deep testing and trials.

Let God comfort you. You don't have to deserve it or perform for it; simply let God be your faith focus. Stay tight with Him. When all hell breaks loose, it is designed to take you down into the cesspools of human despair, to discredit God and, ultimately, for you to die; maybe not physically, but rather by experiencing the death of hope, beauty, and goodness that God had planned to be in your life.

How God can bring back life to dead bones by His mere breath is so amazing! He speaks to the storm, and it calms down. You don't have to understand everything; maybe you never will, but you will get through it if you just keep walking. When there is nothing left in your life to sing about, sing about the mercies of God! Singing will bring light and life in the midst of darkness and death. God not only brings light, but He is light. To Him, darkness and light are the same. Our path is not always crystal clear, but the truth is, even the darkest night is light to God. We are called to walk in faith, which means we keep walking even during those times we cannot see.

His Majesty

Without signing up for it, I was called to walk in places too dark to describe—to move when I had no strength left in my soul. But God was always there; He never once left me nor forsook me! It sometimes takes time along with distance to see true beauty in what we go through. There was no instant gratification: no drive-through meals or easy solutions with "Three Steps to Success." This trial took time, with lots of death moments where things that had no substance, even those in my own heart, burned away. Yet, the last man standing was Jesus Christ in the fullness of His beauty and presence without fail!

Oh, how can I describe His majesty? How can I explain in mere words the warmth of His comfort and power? Just trust me; He is the same yesterday, today, and forever. He is no respecter of persons. Are you afraid of death? Don't be. It's only a door you have not walked through before. Jesus is on the other side with eternal life in a kingdom not of this world. Dear ones, these bodies will all die someday. Flesh cannot stand in the presence of God; death is the bridge to be crossed to bring us, our real selves, safely to His presence.

We are called as followers of Jesus Christ to live by faith; I was about to experience this call in a way I never had before. It was not possible without grace that was amazing and mercies that had no end. I wish I could continue to talk about the beauty and majesty of God, but I must return to the journey that exposed these truths in real life here on earth.

Behold, the LORD's hand is not shortened, that it cannot save;
Nor His ear heavy, that it cannot hear. (Isaiah 59:1)

Even the darkness is not dark to You, and the night is as bright
as the day. Darkness and light are alike to You.
(Psalm 139:12 NASB)

O God, How Much More Could He Endure?

"O my dear God, how can this body be so deep in death yet still be alive?" I cried to God in a moment I'll never forget. Hennie's lean 175-pound body had ballooned to 196 pounds almost overnight due to fluid retention, his body's response to the burn trauma. Swollen from head to toe, he lay trapped in his earthen tent, which was barely able to house the real person any longer. Never in my life had I seen a body and soul so separate while still together. I was very keenly aware that the line between life and death was fading. During the weeks to come, Hennie's life became like a roller coaster ride on a thin thread.

Death was literally at the door, day and night. At one point during the first week, I had this striking moment when I stared at him after his first skin transplant surgery. His body, shaking and wet, smelled like rotting flesh as the cadaver skin that was used to cover the wounds started to decay. The foul smell of dead flesh was the most awful thing to experience, let alone that it was stuck to his body; he could not escape the stench. *Trapped,* that's what he was, trapped in a very broken body.

As I consider those days, I am reminded of how this must be the same with dead works or make-believe Christianity. Spiritually, the odor of that dead flesh must be how hypocrisy and selfish worship smell to God. How awful! The true horror of the situation was he smelled like death, but he was still alive.

The burns became worse before they ever got any better. The shock sustained by his body at the loss of such a substantial part of its largest organ set in at the time of the burn and continued for a long time after. It was like playing a waiting game, waiting to see when things would turn either for the good or the bad. After the initial shock, he had to deal with the plethora of consequences and side effects of the trauma. It seemed like an eternity of waiting for good news, with no one able to tell us that everything was going to be okay.

Even after the skin healed, there was no guarantee that all of the side effects and complications would completely cease. They didn't. He had surgery eleven years later. Some issues will stay with him forever, but they do not impede his quality of life. It now serves as a reminder of the miracles God has done. I remember hearing the doctors voice their concerns that never seemed to change; "He is not out of the woods yet." The exhausting journey went on far too long. Seriously, how much worse was it going to get? Angry and helpless, all we could do was get up, fight, release to God, and repeat.

Among many other functions, the skin was supposed to protect the body's internal tissues and organs that were not created to be exposed to the outside world. The role of the skin to regulate his body's temperature and fight off bacterial invasion was absent, leaving his whole body vulnerable. His breathing became shallow as his whole body shook from shock and cold. His blood work results were all over the place. Hennie's pain, of course, was through the roof, throwing his body into full-blown trauma.

Surgeries and Other Horrible Ways to Healing

The surgeries started several days later. On top of everything that went on, his body had to deal with the anesthesia, adding insult to injury during the skin transplantation process. After surgeries, he would be freezing from his body's lack of temperature control, while the cadaver skin on the wounds had to be kept well hydrated for the best effect. Every three hours the burn staff poured bottles of saline solution over his body to keep the bandages wet. However, his body was unable to regulate his temperature to warm itself. How could we possibly keep a skinless, soaked, weakened body warm? We simply could not.

This issue became a recurring problem after the skin transplant surgeries that followed—like the night he was transported to the operating room to remove the cadaver skin that was failing to serve its purpose. I was so tired that night while driving home, thinking that I'd see him in the morning. However, I received a call from the hospital around 11:00 p.m., and a nurse informed me that Hennie was asking me to come there immediately. I rushed back to the hospital to find him in the worst condition I had yet seen him during this whole ordeal.

I'll Get You Warm

When I got to him, he told me that he was sure he was dying. He was simply too cold to live. He was shaking violently, unable to move or even talk properly. I immediately noticed that he was lying on top of a thick layer of cold, soaking-wet blankets, having no defense against the effect they had on his body. Those blankets were drenched, but no one seemed to realize they were creating a problem for him. With great concern, I immediately asked the staff to get him dry. They responded that his airbed would keep circulating air, eventually drying the blankets and he would be fine. "The transplants have to be kept moist; it's part of the process," I was told.

I knew this was a matter of life and death for Hennie. To me, there was a great difference between *moist* and *soaked*. What were we to care about first? His dying of shock and cold or dying of the transplanted skin's not being kept moist? What a choice! With supernatural boldness and nothing to lose, I demanded action, insisting on getting him dry immediately. I was about to pull those blankets out from underneath him all by myself, figuring out how to do it as I went. The nurse realized there was no stopping me and decided to help. I'll never forget those heavy, ice-cold water- and blood-filled blankets! As it turned out, he had been transferred from the operating room bed—blankets and all—onto his airbed, so he woke up freezing, unable to recover on his own.

The medical team was extraordinarily brave and skillful, fighting hard to save his life, for which I'll be forever grateful. There was always an abundance of activity in the trauma unit where the nurses and technicians did their best to follow doctors' orders very carefully. The doctors examined, operated, performed their procedures, then left until the next time they would do rounds. I cannot count the number of times I requested them to call the doctor about an issue at hand. Without fail, I received great responses with professional follow-up. They had this love-hate relationship with me, but eventually had to realize

I was more helpful than not. I was not going to go away! Thus, they tolerated and accepted me as part of the process to get Hennie well.

We made sure the wounds were moist, getting the rest of his body much drier than before. Still, he could not stop shaking. I got on the bed with him attempting to use my body to help him get warm. Cuddled up with the love of my life, sensing the tentacles of death pulling him away from this world, I held on, praying for relief. My body heat helped a little but not enough.

I finally determined I needed to find a heat lamp or something more to help him get warm. I asked around, but the nurse told me they didn't have heat lamps in the unit. My response? "If there is a heat lamp anywhere in this building, I will hunt it down and bring it back to him." Five minutes later, the staff found an infrared portable lamp. After situating it beside the bed and covering him with heated blankets, I joined him and held him as close to me as possible to provide extra warmth. Heat slowly crept back into his body. To this day Hennie will tell you that night was one of the worst nights of his life, and he has had some dire ones.

Red Carpet

Medical staff members are angels, yet the worst place to be when you are really sick is in a hospital! Death hovers, and disease-causing germs thrive there, so having someone healthy, feisty, and godly with you in times of serious illness is highly recommended. I had great appreciation and consideration for the staff and valued my interaction with them, but my primary mission was to get Hennie comfortable and well. Second on my priority list was getting along with the staff. I found doing so to be a very delicate dance. I had to reach deep into my soul to remain wisely gracious in negotiating and interacting with the medical team. I had to build a relationship of trust, while at the same time demanding attention. Sometimes I feared being asked to leave!

At one point, I was called to a meeting with the doctors, nurses, and psychiatrists who tried to get me to back off from Hennie's care and not be there all of the time. To them a wife's hovering over her sick husband in this way was not normal. Their assessment was that I felt guilty because Hennie was so sick and hopeless, while I was healthy and well. The team tried to help me understand that all this was not my fault. I should go on with my life while they did their jobs to get Hennie well. I finally realized they were concerned about me while I was totally oblivious, thinking I was doing what anyone would have done for a loved one.

Their psychoanalysis of me was futile, of course. With the favor of God, I was able to convince them I was part of the solution—not the problem. They decided to accept my determination to help with his care. As time went on, the nurses let me know they appreciated my help. They had their hands full with all their sick patients, so I became a normal part of Hennie's daily care.

Absolutely Not!

I soon found that I had a battle to fight on multiple fronts at the same time during Hennie's hospitalization. My husband was dying, I was still a mom to a beautiful little girl, I had to stay in good standing with the staff, huge hospital bills started accumulating, and on and on. I experienced firsthand that Satan is no gentleman. He pounces on the weak, being broken and distraught is not enough, sure death and final destruction is his only satisfaction. Well, his lack of consideration made me angry!

So this became my resolution: watch out because I'm not giving in, letting up, or stepping back! I've got God on my side. Along with my perceived ignorance came weapons that are not of this world but mighty in God to pull down strongholds inhabited by any demon from hell! God is far greater!

Skin Transplants

No skin remained on his body but a small section on the back of his shoulders, which could be retrieved to use for transplants on the third-degree burns. Technology has advanced greatly since, but at the time of his accident the only procedure for a permanent solution to third-degree burns was to use the person's own skin for transplant or leave it, of course, waiting for the wound to gradually grow smaller until the areas covered over with new skin. Waiting was a prolonged process and posed a great danger of infection. Of course, developing an infection would have made the wounds worse, preventing healthy skin growth and could have spread to other parts of Hennie's body with dire consequences.

He started to heal from the surgeries with brand-new skin growing back over the once raw flesh. I eagerly examined his body every day to see if the wounds were getting smaller. It was an incredibly slow process, though, so the risk of infection loomed with no end. I learned to rejoice over any pink speck of flesh that was not there the day before. Any sign of life or growth was what I lived to see each day to match the faith in my heart that he was going to fully recover. This is where some people must have thought I was crazy, but to walk in faith you can't avoid crazy at times!

Second-degree burns, on the other hand, still have some skin cells in the burn area. The skin grows from the bottom up instead of from the sides inward, as is the case with third-degree burns. The vast areas of second-degree burns needed to be scrubbed several times every 24 hours to remove any dead cells that could cause infection. Third-degree areas had no skin cells with all of the layers burned away, including the nerves. However, in second-degree burns, all of the nerves remained intact to absorb the slightest insult from the outside. A sign of health in the second-degree burns was a bright pinkish color that indicated proper blood supply and skin growth. Brown areas of pus were unwelcome news, requiring removal either by scrubbing or being surgically cut away under anesthesia.

During the weeks that followed the accident, he had multiple surgeries to transplant skin to the areas most affected by the burns. At first, they used cadaver skin which lasted around five days, giving the skin some protection and an opportunity to grow. It also gave Hennie's lesser burned skin a chance to recover, so it could be used for future transplants. Initially, he had no unharmed skin anywhere on his body that could have been used in a transplant, so using cadaver skin was the only option.

Eventually he was ready for skin transplants with his own skin. During the surgery, the surgeons would shave off the good skin, leaving behind another second-degree burn in that area. The shaved-off skin was then perforated in a machine that would allow it to stretch to cover a larger area of the wounds. Most of his transplants were successful, as his body recognized its own skin; new skin soon grew in those areas. In the process of treatment, not all the transplants took to the body one hundred percent, but we were grateful for every bit of success toward his recovery.

I find it somewhat comical that Hennie has freckles on his legs now. The few freckles he had on his shoulders were transplanted to his legs! Yes, it's amazing how the body works. The freckles from his shoulders remained when the skin was transplanted to his legs. At least now both of us have freckles on our legs. How cool is that? I'm no longer the only one with freckles!

The Leg Story

Talking about his legs, allow me to share the full leg story! I have been accused of falling for his perfectly created athletic legs when we first met, which was, of course, totally untrue. Yet, accused I stood. In my judgment, the man always had "killer legs." Even after all he has gone through, he still has the most handsome legs this side of heaven! Me, on the other hand, not so much. I've always had a complex about my legs for reasons better left alone.

One day during that first week following the accident, I went home for a shower to put on fresh clothes. As I was looking down at my bare legs, I was shocked. For the first time in my entire life, I stared at my legs in admiration of their perfection and beauty. They had skin! They were perfect! Amazing how perspective can change everything when nothing else changes!

Back in the hospital, Hennie's perfect legs were suffering greatly. I remember the first time the nurses allowed me in the room when the bandages were being taken off to prepare him for the scrubbing session. I felt sick to my stomach. I thought I was going to throw up but managed to keep it together because I had to. The bandages would stick to the raw flesh every time they had to be removed for the scrubbing baths. The raw wounds would ooze blood and other fluids. More skin peeled off his body every time the bandages were being removed. The bandages had to be wet to be able to remove them, but even with the ointment between the burns and bandages, pieces of tissue from the already suffering flesh were ripped from his body along with the bandages. Hennie would groan from pain, begging us to remove them as slowly as possible. Later, the nurses allowed me to start removing the bandages well ahead of time, so I could do it more slowly to eliminate some of the pain. How he ever got through those times, I'll never know, but by the grace of God, he did!

You Don't Use It; You Lose It

A week or so after the accident, his body was becoming so weak that he was unable to pick up his Bible. He could not lift it off the tray in front of him as he was very fragile, shaking all the time. He couldn't even feed himself. One day the medical team decided he had to try to stand up from the bed to get his body moving. With much trouble, we finally got him on his feet next to his bed as several of us held him upright. The next moment we noticed he was standing in a pool of fresh blood. It took us a minute to realize it was his own blood.

Under the weight of his body, the pressure of standing up was too much for the newly formed veins in his legs: blood flooded from the veins through the bandages onto the floor. Literally, a pool of blood formed on the floor where he was standing, so we got him back in bed immediately.

The flames had completely annihilated some blood vessels, but the body is an amazing machine. The veins grew back exactly where they needed to be. At first, they were as thin as paper and extremely fragile, but over time they grew into healthy, fully formed veins. The healing was amazing to behold.

It was usually quite a process of maneuvering pillows and blankets to get him comfortable in bed. Discomfort was painful; it could have caused more skin damage. The goal was to get him out of pain because sleep was necessary for his body to rejuvenate and grow some skin! Sleep—what a novel idea in the burn trauma unit where slumber or sleep tempt death, yet, it is still needed by even the sickest of bodies.

Now Also Losing His Mind?

After a week of 24-hour days where there were no nights but around-the-clock constant care, Hennie became combative and disoriented. He started hallucinating, scheming plans to go home. He gave me detailed plots on how I was to smuggle him out of the hospital. He pointed to a wheelchair in the hallway that we could use for our escape in the middle of the night. He insisted that they were trying to kill him in that tub. He needed to get away and was fully convinced that I could give him all the care he needed at home. He even configured how I was to help him get in and out of the shower at home.

The man has always had a brilliant mind, but now he was losing it. The schemes were quite well contrived though. I had my hands full simply trying to calm him down. In the meanwhile, I promised him that we would follow his plan as soon as the coast was clear on some dark night when no one was looking. That night never came, of course, but I had to get into his world as much as I could in order to help him get through it.

He also asked the nurses to call Tessa. He talked with her on the phone, asking if he could come live with them rather than stay in the hospital. That must have been a tough conversation for Tessa to convince him that it was not possible.

Have We Both Lost It?

That was the point at which I also started to lose some of my judgment—or maybe most of it. Dr. Nuss was a dear and close friend, as well as a physician. One night in desperation, I asked him to be Hennie's doctor from that day forth. I was going to fire the whole team of specialists working with Hennie and find a way for him to officially become Hennie's primary care doctor as well as medical team leader. I told him we'd do anything to make it happen.

Why not? He was, and still is, one of the smartest people you'd ever meet in ten lifetimes, so he could figure it out, right? After all, taking care of a burn patient is almost the same as doing surgery on infants—well, maybe not, because he was a pediatric surgeon and not a plastic surgeon or anything remotely related to treating burn patients. What was I thinking? And the bigger question is what was Dr. Nuss thinking?

It did not matter to me what anyone thought of me during that time. *Dr. Nuss comes to see Hennie every day anyway,* I thought. *He could just as well be his doctor!* The transfer of doctors never happened, but Dr. Nuss was a trusted friend and ally in the battle for Hennie's life. He is a Christian man filled with the Spirit of God, and I trust him with my life. I believe God worked through him, as He often does, to bring Hennie some relief. During his brief visit with Hennie the next day, concerned about Hennie's hallucinations and ingenious schemes to escape from the hospital, he asked the staff, "How much sleep has Hennie had during the past week?"

The answer?

"None. No sleep."

Dr. Nuss immediately understood the implications and conferred with Hennie's doctors to help him get some sleep. They realized that the lack of sleep on top of the trauma, surgeries and strong medication was taking its toll on Hennie's mind. Several hours of good sleep made a huge difference, so we thanked God for the breakthrough.

Oh how I thank God for the small miracles that happened all the time and eventually added up to one big miracle of wonderful restoration! No matter the circumstances, small miracles happen around us all of the time while we often wait for the big ones. Not seeing the small ones causes us to lose hope and gratefulness, which are crucial to staying alive in mind, body, and spirit.

How About You?

All of these physical, medical, and scientific facts are lessons of spiritual truths at play in our lives every day. Sometimes things in our lives have to get worse before they'll ever get any better. Hard decisions often need to be made and harsh treatment applied in order to get healthy again. When a heart is broken or a life ruined, simply letting it be and hoping for the best will not make things better for the most part. Be courageous, take action, and get well. Perhaps a relationship that needs to end or forgiveness extended to restore a broken one needs your attention. Tough love is part of life, and doing the right and godly thing does not always feel good. At least, not for the moment.

Many people walk around with major spiritual wounds and injuries, unable to help themselves. At times in life, we have to accept help from someone else. God wants to restore us back to a close relationship with Him, heal grieving hearts, and redeem us from the darkness of tormenting fear. This restoration can be paralyzing, but it is crucial to find someone with whom to link your faith, someone who can pray with you and encourage you to find your way back to God. Don't delay; it is never too late.

Carnal thoughts and self-serving activities produce death to the spirit, just as ingratitude in the smallest victories produces a life void of joy and celebration. The worst possible reaction to pain and disappointment is anger. Choosing this reaction leaves you powerless, gives room for matters to fester, and leads to questioning God, which annihilates hope from the human soul.

Instead of choosing anger, get help, get with God and get on the road to recovery! God's will is for you to live a beautiful satisfying life, so don't settle for anything less. We all go through seasons of darkness, but we don't have to stay there. Let us enforce our God-given spiritual authority over darkness and seeming defeat by living above the circumstances. The road to healing is always a humbling one. You may bleed, have to ask for help, feel like you are losing your mind, be misunderstood, but keep walking and keep believing. It will prove to be well worth it in the end. You are not alone.

4

The Power of Moments

Celebrating Good Moments Even When Life Hurts

A T THE MOMENT OF the accident, Hennie held a small container with gasoline in his right hand. He was using the gas to prime the carburetor to help start our stranded vehicle. The carburetor backfired, instantly igniting the gasoline. In the shock of the explosion, the flaming gasoline spilled on his clothing and exposed flesh.

Save the Fingers!

His right hand took the first spill of burning gas. Then it showered his bare legs. The blazing flames burned his clothing right off his body. The top of his right hand suffered one of the worst third-degree burns his body received. Burned to the bones, all of the layers of tissue were destroyed—even the veins in that area.

I remember the doctors telling me that night that no blood supply was reaching the fingers of his hand and that they might have to amputate the fingers. *Those are his fingers,* I thought. *There's no way anything else is going to be cut off of his body on top of what has already burned off!*

I went to the public phone in the hospital hallway and called everyone I could reach to ask them to pray for his fingers to come back to life. I knew prayer was what we needed at that moment for his fingers to somehow be saved and for the blood flow to get all the way to the tips. We would deal with the rest of the life-threatening issues later, but in that moment, we wanted his fingers to live. It would have been easy, at least understandable, to amputate the fingers and do whatever was needed under the circumstances as long as he was alive and not dead. But no, we wanted his life to be with his fingers!

Committing Good Moments to Memory

It's amazing how life can change in a moment of time. Everything can literally change in the blink of an eye. But I hope none of my loved ones or friends, or anyone reading this book, will ever have to experience change in the way we did. Life happens in moments and is remembered in moments, so when life presents you good moments, grab them with all your might. Do whatever it takes to celebrate them. Bad moments that create bad memories without invitation happen all by themselves.

The nature of traumatic experiences is that they burn a pathway in your brain for future recurrence or recollection of the pain. Somehow good moments do not always have that same effect, possibly because the pain of the bad is oftentimes much more intense than the joy of the good. One of the ways in which this theory is evident to me is according to the answers my kids give me when I ask them about their favorite family vacation memories while growing up. They easily recall the stories of how we were rained out of our tent in Canada one summer and spent a day in a laundromat drying out our bedding and tent for the next night, or the flea-infested motel with the worn-out beds and the bees at the swimming pool in Florida one year. They vividly recall the upstate New York border patrol who said they'd let us into Canada, but not back into the US, since we didn't have our resident alien cards with us. How about the times the kids got punished for something they were not guilty of committing?

What about the many trips in our beautiful, almost brand-new, 28-foot motorhome when they were growing up? The one we could not really afford. For the sake of creating fun and memorable childhood experiences for our family, we bought it anyway. We crossed the country and enjoyed many trips, including visits to the Grand Canyon, Yellowstone National Park, Mount Rushmore, Yosemite National Park, the Blue Ridge Mountains, Niagara Falls, Disney World, Epcot, and even the French Quarter in New Orleans. What about all those times? They periodically assure me that the vast majority of their childhood memories are wonderful, but I have found listening to memories of the bad ones can easily get me depressed. We worked so hard to create countless wonderful childhood memories for them, so I see it as my obligation to often recall the good stories so they will not forget.

Build Monuments for Your Family

For the same reasons, God had His people build monuments and observe recurrent feasts in biblical times. God wanted to remind His people of the good times, as well as the God encounters in their lives. God is so serious about the power of remembering and celebrating good moments that He not only teaches us to celebrate our own good experiences, but also for us to teach the generations to come to continue the celebrations. Why? Because we are so apt to forget His goodness when this life, with its many struggles, easily overshadows us like a big dark cloud.

We need to work on not missing the beautiful everyday moments by remembering the goodness of God toward us. If we allow them to, bad moments and experiences will trump every good moment we are granted in this life and leave us miserable and ungrateful.

Mastering this skill as early in life as possible is crucial. Learn to celebrate both the big and small events of life. Don't miss an opportunity to reminisce about past fun, enjoyable times, and other good moments. Laugh with those who laugh so that difficult, tearful times don't find you empty and alone.

Trauma in the human soul has tremendous power to ingrain the pain into permanent thinking patterns. Those can become default pathways by which to measure everything and everyone in life, leaving us expecting the worst in every situation and person. Pain could ruin the rest of your life; it surely threatened our future in many ways.

Miracles Upon Miracles

The possible loss of Hennie's fingers was one of the first smaller battles to fight. We watched as God restored the blood flow to his fingers at what seemed to be the eleventh hour—just in time to save them from being amputated. Wow! His fingers were going to survive! How amazing! That miracle boosted our faith for the coming days, weeks, and months to believe God for the next miracle. Each miracle seemed to make room for the next battle or threat that needed to be overcome. The journey was exhausting and didn't seem to stop for a long, long time.

We tackled one crisis at a time. Whatever was on the menu of the day's victories that had to be won received our full attention and fight. I thank God for the many people who prayed for us during that time. Hennie's fellow students at Regent University contacted their churches, the prayer teams they knew, and family members all over the globe to pray for him. We received cards and messages from believers near and far who assured us that they were praying and standing with us.

I could never in a million years have understood or calculated the full value and power of all the prayers that were prayed for Hennie's healing. So many of them were answered. I know that is what sustained and strengthened him for the fight. Additionally, those prayers set many enemies to flight at many different times. I was acutely aware of the support of the saints during that time. We cherish the endless memories of people God sent to hold up our arms.

Words Are Much More Than Mere Communication

One battle at a time, which is all we had strength for, became part of our everyday life. I had no luxury to think that tomorrow was going to be a better day, but I found myself unable to even think of the next day or hour. The next hour on any given day could have been bad, so God's grace kept me in the moment. All I could do was to breathe one breath at a time. It kept me alive as well as in faith for that moment.

Every time Hennie pulled oxygen into his lungs, while lying in that bed of death, was a moment he was alive. I was so grateful for those moments—for any signs of life.

One day the room was quiet for a change. Hennie was trying to recover from the previous scrubbing and dressing changes. He was all clean and wrapped up, lying in his bed, while the nurses were busy elsewhere. I climbed up on the back of the chair next to his bed for a better vantage point to look down on his body.

I stared at him. I had no words and could not think really well either. I focused on God in an effort to confirm in my heart that He was there with us. I wanted to pray but could not find words. I wanted to quote Scripture but actually felt too weak to come up with anything in and of myself. All I could muster up that day was to pick up the Bible and open to the book of Psalms—any psalm.

I started to read one psalm after the other out loud. I loved the sound of reading the verses. It said what needed to be said—what I could not say at the time. I clung to every word, and infusions of power from heaven came into that room. The moment was miraculous and remains forever etched in my spirit. Words of life were spoken through the weakest of instruments ever.

What started as mere words turned into declarations and prophesies over his body that had no hope outside of Jesus Christ. I had nothing. Hennie had nothing. Neither of us had anything to bring to the table—not even one prayer or Scripture to recite, but we had the Word of God in our hearts and hands, which saved our lives that day. Giving voice and sound to the Word of God enforced the authority of God in the situation. Reading it aloud brought it to life, appropriating its power like the very day it was spoken by God.

When God speaks, the words work for eternity. They never fall to the ground and never stop or go away. His Word is alive and powerful forever. That day God gave favor to my feeble contribution of speaking

His mighty, powerful words. How can we ever understand this mystery and out-of-this-world truth? Only by faith, and therefore we are called to live by faith. The battle is for our faith. The Bible calls it a fight of faith. I had been tempted that day to simply let go of hope and life and give up, but God rescued me through His Word.

I realize I cannot paint the full picture of the majesty of God. It is only to be found by each one of us individually for full revelation and truth. Even now, the more I express my experience with God and His hand of power, the more limited I am in describing or communicating His majesty. God is so big and unfathomable, yet as God, He invites us to build a relationship with Him that is personal and powerful. His words are truly pure and experiencing it is much more powerful than merely knowing it. We often experience God more when we are weak—whether in running to God or even blaming God. Either way, it is not wrong to feel weak. In many societies weakness is not tolerated or admitted, which is sad, for it is in our times of weakness we find the strength of God that changes our lives.

Let go of all the things you think you know and have figured out, and only look at Jesus. In His presence and words are the answers to life, goodness, and success. For me, our journey was a place in God's presence I'd rather not have experienced, but it is a treasure beyond earthly value that will keep my heart until I see Jesus face to face.

Who has ascended into heaven, or descended? Who has gathered the wind in His fists? Who has bound the waters in a garment? Who has established all the ends of the earth? What is His name, and what is His Son's name, If you know?

Every word of God is pure; He is a shield to those who put their trust in Him. (Proverbs 30:4-5)

Mother and Son

Yet another night came for me to take one last look at my husband, not knowing if he would stay alive till the next day. I had something to look forward to that night, though, because my mother-in-law had arrived from South Africa. She came to see her son and help me take care of Yolandie and the house. Our reunion was emotional but good, and we made plans to go see Hennie the first thing the next morning. Nothing could have prepared me for the moment she walked into her son's room and saw him for the first time after the accident. There he was, sitting up in a chair, trying his hardest to be strong for the occasion. The nurses had purposely gotten him out of bed to wait for his mom to show her that he was able to sit up.

He was literally skin and bones. Once the swelling in his body subsided, all of his muscle tone was gone. That day in that chair he was not even able to hold his mouth closed—his mouth hung open as he struggled to hold up his head. His feet touched the floor but shook up and down like someone riding a bicycle on a dirt road. His arms hung limply next to him as if they were lame. I don't know what was going through his mind at that time—who would ever know? He was a pitiful sight indeed.

Hennie looked at his mom in a way that I just knew he was glad to see her. He could not respond as she walked over to him. It took a moment for her to find a way to hug or touch him before she took his head in her hands to talk into his ear. She told him that she was so happy to see him, assuring him that she was there to help make things better. Oh, what a godly woman! What a moment in time!

This greeting was in stark contrast to the first greeting I ever witnessed between the two of them years before. He was taking me to introduce me to his mom and his family, and we finally arrived in Potchefstroom after eighteen hours on the road from Cape Town. It was early evening as we drove up the long driveway past the house to the garage in the backyard. I didn't see where his mom came from. I could only surmise it must have been from the back door of the house. But by the time I got out of the passenger side of the car and looked over to his side of the car, she had grabbed him in an embrace that wouldn't let go. They held each other for what seemed a long time to me—definitely too long—I was not used to that kind of greeting. Besides, I was the guest, yet initially I didn't receive any attention from her at all.

I have three brothers and had a wonderful saint for a mom. She also was happy to see any of her sons after a time of separation, but her joy at seeing any of her children was nothing like what I was seeing. When you see the bond between mother and son and know it is not your ordinary mom-and-son relationship, you know you are seeing the holy moments of life. Hennie's mom had seen him go through a great deal of sadness in his young life, which may have been the reason why they were so close. The bonding after his birth following the loss of her husband was the start of a connection between them that was very special. It remained that way till the last time they saw each other.

She used to tell me how her girlfriends prayed with her for Hennie while he was serving in the military. He was on the front lines in the South African Army at a time when many soldiers were frequently lost in combat. She told me how she spent her evenings in prayer and intercession, pleading the shielding power of the blood of Jesus over her son. She was convinced, and so became I, that the hand of God through those prayers brought him back home safely after serving his country.

She also walked with him, unlike any of her other four kids, through the valley of the shadow of death when Hennie buried his young wife and baby who both died as a result of complications during pregnancy. Mom and baby were doing well up to about six weeks prior to her due date, when she suddenly suffered a massive aneurysm. In an effort to save her life, they also lost the precious, perfect little baby boy. Hennie's family rallied around him as he had to bury two of his beloved people in his life, together with all his hopes and dreams of their future. His mom was there for him once again, praying him through a tragic time of grief.

I forever count it a privilege to be his wife and to honor the lives and memories of a truly beautiful godly woman as well as a perfect little boy who did not find a place in this world any longer. They are with Jesus. I can't imagine the pain this brought to her family and also to Hennie.

Hennie's mom was a brave, seasoned woman who brought strength, hope and relief to our situation. She took over the duties at home: I came home every night to a cooked meal, a clean home, an empty laundry basket, and a happy little two-year-old princess! She and Yolandie were two peas in a pod. She adored her granddaughter! I'm sure she would have given her life for that little girl if she were called to do so. She taught me how to be strong and courageous, and if I could be half the woman she was, I'd be happy.

Her Last Goodbye

It's appropriate to also tell you about their last and final time together. In June of 2014, Hennie and I went to South Africa to celebrate the birthdays of both of our mothers. They were turning 90 years old in June and July of that year. We only had one day with his mom as it required travel by plane and road to get to her following thirty hours of traveling to South Africa. Though we had limited time away from home in the USA, we treasured every moment.

His mom was living in a care facility where she had her own small room in a hallway of rooms with strangers who all became her friends. She was mobile and walked without a walker, held a very cerebral conversation, ate well, laughed, and enjoyed our visit. Hennie's sister brought the tea, cakes, and pastries we all enjoyed as we spent time with her in the big living room in the home. We took turns to visit with her individually and had time to catch up on the many years we spent apart as a family. His sister and I noticed how Hennie was sitting with his mom on the couch, close to her with his arm around her shoulder.

They were in deep conversation, clearly enjoying each other's company, as they talked and laughed together. What a beautiful sight that was! I know my husband, and I knew he needed to touch her, hold her, and give her his full and complete attention. We let him take all the time he needed, trying not to interrupt any of this beautiful connection they enjoyed. They had so much love and honor for each other. I'll never forget that visit as long as I live. It turned out to be their final visit this side of heaven—a moment to treasure forever. They had been separated from each other for most of their lives, which must have been hard for this mother. I know the separation was hard for Hennie, for sure.

She died that September.

Back in the USA at our Thanksgiving table the following month, I read him this adaptation of Proverbs 31 when it was my turn in our tradition to give thanks. I wrote this to him during my time with God earlier that week on November 23, 2014. He was so moved by what I read that he told our family around the table that God knew he needed it. While listening to me read it, he felt comforted in the loss of his mother. This is my rendering of Proverbs 31 dedicated to Hennie. To give the "husband" version of this very familiar piece of Scripture, he was on my mind with every line I wrote.

My Proverbs 31 Husband

Who can find a brave husband? His worth is far above that of houses and lands.

The heart of his wife is at peace in knowing she is safe.

He protects and comforts her, never leaves her out in the rain, all the days of her life.

He diligently pursues to prosper, to provide plentifully for his family.

He is like a stealth fighter; swiftly flying to fulfill his mission and bring home the victory.

He also sleeps soundly by night to gain strength, to fill his wife's hands with plenty for his own house and that of another.

He plans, plants seeds, works with the sweat of his brow, waters it and patiently waits for its abundant fruit.

He bravely opens his heart to the ones he loves, making himself vulnerable in his strength.

He perceives that his home is in order and happily eats and relishes the fruit of his sacrifices.

He stretches out his hands into the unknown and doesn't waiver in darkness or danger.

He extends his hand to the weak; he's never too strong to be tender.

He is not afraid of drought for his household, but stored up water when no one noticed.

He fixes anything that is broken; his home doesn't leak when it rains.

His wife is known in the marketplace, where she buys fields to profit her house and that of the needy.

He studies and works hard to show himself approved and brings wisdom and gain to those who accompany him.

Strength and honor are his breastplate as he proudly brings hope for the future.

He opens his mouth with direction and instruction and has the power to speak freedom and blessing to his home.

He delights in the maturing of his household and protects it with his life.

His children rise up and call him brave, his wife also, and she praises him.

Many sons have done well, but you are better than all of them together.

Charisma is deceitful and pride a trap, but a man who fears the
Lord shall reap honor.

Give him the fruit of his hands, and let his life speak into generations to come.

How About You?

To all the young ones, I want to say again, life is remembered in
moments—mere moments. There are bad, better, and good—as well
as great—moments in life. Life is not bad because of bad moments,
but rather because of a lack of good moments. Sometimes the good
moments are not recognized but get away without being celebrated.
Other times you may simply not have enough good moments to sustain you during the bad ones. Make beautiful memories whenever you
can and don't underestimate the power of joyous times, even if they
seem small. Some day you will find out those were the big things in
life. It will be too late then, and there is no way in which to recoup
those losses.

It's never too late to start new traditions that honor and celebrate
people and events in life. It does not have to be elaborate to be mean-
ingful. Start with the obvious, like birthdays and holidays. Every day is
special, but we can't have a party every day, so grab the obvious reasons
to celebrate and acknowledge the occasion.

Many of my fondest childhood memories are connected to routine
celebrations ranging from birthdays to rainy days, special Saturday
morning breakfasts to after-church visits on Sunday nights. Memories
of good moments keep important influences alive in our hearts; they
are something to believe in and serve as examples to follow.

What about the horrible and terrible memories and moments? I
read a statistic about marriages that claims that divorce does not hap-

pen because of bad things in relationships, rather the lack of good ones. I'm not sure if that statistic is totally true, but from all my experience over many years of helping married couples find the way to successful relationships, I believe it is fairly accurate.

Painful events are often extremely hard to overcome and the truth is that the effects may never go away completely. The key is to leave them where they belong—behind you. Create good memories and be the beauty to your world. Soon you'll have more than enough for which to be grateful and to celebrate.

This is a moment in time in your life. Don't let it slip away. Make good memories and help them last.

Let us go celebrate something!

5

About Hell

Redefining What It Means to Win in Life

As I was running across the street with flames burning all over my body, all I could think was I have to tell everyone that hell is no joke, but real and more painful than anyone can imagine!

– Hennie

Hell is real.

Eternity is long.

God is merciful.

This would be a good time to stop reading if this book is merely about someone else's story to you—especially if you want to continue to feel safe and comfortable in the bubble of your own carefully crafted belief system. That bubble will burst—it's only a matter of time—because life is bigger than any one person. God is Ruler over all. His ways are much higher than any man's, for this life is much more than what we see and feel right now.

There is a whole world and a system in the unseen realm that affects all of us every day, but most of the time we don't realize it or know about it. The truth beyond what seems obvious to us in this physical world is that a higher order and another world than what we experience in this dispensation of time exists. God wants us not to be ignorant people, but ones who are brave enough to explore the whole truth according to God, our Creator. Allow Him to speak to you through His Word, the Bible.

Whoever loves instruction loves knowledge, But he who hates correction is stupid. (Proverbs 12:1)

Why Talk About Hell?

This chapter is not for the faint of heart or anyone who is not ready to face the truth, but it is a crucial part of this story. This is not make-believe; it is real life. Hennie is a real person with a real body that burned with real fire followed by suffering real destruction. Many people suffer all over the world every minute of every day; people die somewhere each second we breathe, suffering and death is nothing new. Hopefully, our unique personal story may encourage some weary, heartbroken soul somewhere to revive a flickering of hope.

What Hennie experienced and suffered was here on earth but serves as a reminder of a greater truth according to God's Word. The Bible teaches us how physical laws in this world are shadows as well as lessons in the realities of the unseen spiritual world where God and other spiritual beings operate. Let's not get lost in the theological arguments, but be wise as God's will is for us to understand the spiritual world and eternal life, which is scripturally inseparable from hell and eternal judgment.

And don't forget Sodom and Gomorrah and their neighboring towns, which were filled with immorality and every kind of sexual perversion. Those cities were destroyed by fire and serve as a warning of the eternal fire of God's judgment. (Jude 1:7 NLT)

Jesus Christ is the same yesterday, today, and forever.
(Hebrews 13:8)

If you think the Bible talks about hell in figurative and not literal speech, do you think figurative will hurt any less? Do you really think you should only be concerned about what hurts physically? What hurts more, a broken bone or a broken heart? Think about it. The Scriptures, in whatever dispensation of time, speak of pain, suffering, and judgment outside of our known world and time. For eternity! Whatever form it will take we may not be able to understand right now, but it will happen. Jesus would not have repeatedly referred to hell if the place had no implication or was a figment of His or our imagination or was inconsequential to us here on earth. The following are warnings and prophecies everyone should hear and understand.

> *Just as the weeds are sorted out and burned in the fire, so it will be at the end of the world. The Son of Man will send his angels, and they will remove from his Kingdom everything that causes in and all who do evil. And the angels will throw them into the fiery furnace, where there will be weeping and gnashing of teeth. Then the righteous will shine like the sun in their Father's Kingdom. Anyone with ears to hear should listen and understand!*
> (Matthew 13:40-43 NLT)

> *"Then the king will turn to those on the left and say, 'Away with you, you cursed ones, into the eternal fire prepared for the devil and his demons.'"* (Matthew 25:41 NLT)

> *But cowards, unbelievers, the corrupt, murderers, the immoral, those who practice witchcraft, idol worshipers, and all liars— their fate is in the fiery lake of burning sulfur. This is the second death.* (Revelation 21:8 NLT)

> *If your hand causes you to sin, cut it off. It is better for you to enter into life maimed, rather than having two hands, to go to hell, into the fire that shall never be quenched.* (Mark 9:43)

This chapter is not a theological thesis about hell. I fully understand many interpretations exist on this subject, yet it is wise to consider several facts.

First of all, the thought of hell with its description is terribly brutal and harsh. Yes, it must be something awful that Jesus saved us from by dying a horrendous death on the cross! If it were true, would you not want to know?

Second, some say that since God is a loving God, such a place of punishment is out of character for Him. Not so much if you look at the Old Testament, which speaks of God as "a man of war." He is also just, merciful, and in love with mankind, offering us a way out through the suffering of His own Son, Jesus Christ.

Third, your church or denomination may teach that there is no hell, no punishment, no separation from God here on earth and/or in eternity. If theology or theological teachings could fix mankind or save the world, we'd all be happily living in a perfect world or heaven right now. It would also have saved Jesus from dying in order to save us. That is clearly not the case—neither scripturally nor experientially.

Much has been studied and written about God's character, ways, laws and plans, but none of that has ever saved anyone. Only by Jesus Christ can anyone be saved. He is the Son of the living God, the Creator of the universe, Sustainer of life in all things seen and unseen.

This is not an interesting article or a feel-good devotional, but a story of how love saved my husband from certain death by flames. Essentially, this story of love is all of our stories. Hennie could not do or contribute anything to secure his survival, but God's and my love for him manifested powerfully when he was too weak and feeble to even ask for it—just like we were before Jesus gave His life as a ransom for our freedom from hell and damnation.

So unless you are searching for answers, meaning, comfort, truth, and freedom for your soul, you'll be disappointed in what I'm about to address. Please keep reading though. Open your heart to God—not to me. Decide for yourself.

Fire

God knows this is something I do not want to talk about, but I am compelled to share this. It is gross, but was real, and just as the breath of God brought life back to what was burned away in Hennie's body, He wants to bring back life to whatever is dead in your life. This topic is probably better left alone, but after our first-hand experience of this unthinkable event, we must address it.

Bloody and Raw

Nothing is more grossly destructive to flesh than fire! Hennie's body was alive and perfectly well one moment, yet destroyed the next. If you've had a loved one die as the result of fire, I am convinced it took only seconds for them to lose consciousness. In that sense, death was a welcome end to immense suffering should your loved one have survived. Hennie teetered on the brink of death, but it was not his time to die.

No other description fit his wounds but that of raw, bloody meat. White, lifeless pieces of flesh and skin covered his body, where the flames had left behind no visible signs of life. The mixture of pink, white, and yellow shreds of living and dead flesh looked like someone had used pliers to rip his skin to shreds. The sight was unrecognizably disturbing.

Yes, the word *fire* was never meant to be used in the same sentence with *human flesh*. Its effect on the human body is probably best described as hellish. Demonic. Evil. It brings utter destruction to something so beautifully and wonderfully created. Fire destroyed the life in Hennie's skin, as well as some of the underlying tissues and muscle. It was here one moment, gone the next. After the fire had devoured the skin on his legs, its flames kept licking at the tissues until some of his calf muscles were also devoured. Seemingly, fire is never satisfied while any signs of life still remain, for as long as it burns, it eats and destroys everything in its path of doom. The same devouring happened on the top of one hand; the flesh was burned away to the bone. Seeing the ruin flames leave behind on a human body is absolutely a most horrific sight.

At this point, allow me to share another very personal, but powerful, detail about the effect of the flames on his body about which you may have wondered. As the flames spread from the burning gasoline on his skin to the clothes he was wearing, they seemed to melt from his body. During the burn, he ripped off all of his clothes, and crazy as it may seem, the pure cotton underwear he wore did not burn! We only realized this afterward upon a closer examination of his injuries. The flames and gasoline burned his skin and clothes but stopped spreading beyond the elastic bands of his underwear. Seemingly, a clear boundary had been drawn for how far the flames were allowed to go—just as if God had draw a line because He still had plans for Hennie's future. Hennie carried the seed of a promise yet to be fulfilled. Wow! Yes, how crazy is that?! I knew in my heart that some people would want to know this detail, so there! God blessed us with two more sons after this whole ordeal, and Niel and Heinz are living memorials of our miracle from heaven.

When I recall all these scenes of raw flesh along with what I know about hell, the picture quickly becomes very dark, fitting perfectly the description of hell in the Bible. There will be moaning, groaning, gnashing of teeth, and a pool of fire that never stops burning. Considering the reality of hell as the destination of some people is extremely disturbing to me! According to the Bible, the redemptive blood of Jesus Christ on a life is the only saving alternative. Disturbing. It seems far easier to avoid or even dismiss this alternative to hell—the redemptive blood of Christ—yet it is God's Word and needs to be taken seriously.

What Is That Smell?

Then there was the smell I shared about earlier—the smell of burned flesh. It is as if the very force of hell zaps all signs of life of the flesh into oblivion—simply eating it up, leaving the body with the stench that makes a person want to vomit. The smell of death—unearthly, inhumane!

As I stood at his bedside in that hospital room, I will never forget that smell, but there was nothing I could do about it. I have a personal thing about smells, and I guess I'm very blessed in that area. Smelling beautiful perfume or even food flavors evokes deep emotions inside of me and can literally transport me to another time and place. I love perfume; what can I say? I always tell Hennie, "If you can't take me to Paris, just get me some great perfume, and it will take me there." I know this is not the same for everyone, but someday I may write a book on smells—physical and spiritual. So you can imagine how the smell of death sat over me like a cloud from hell. I felt that the devil was mocking me with every breath I took.

Just when I thought Hennie's ordeal could not get worse, it did. The smell of dead and rotting tissue must be the big brother of the smell of burned flesh. Even though his wounds were scrubbed several times a day, those scrubbings the first couple of days did not remove all of burned tissue, and it started to smell horribly. The grafted cadaver skin initially used started rotting and smelling within the first 24 hours following surgery. It's amazing how someone else's skin can serve as an emergency dressing for a brief time, the body is smart enough to realize it's from another source and goes into full blown rejection of the foreign cells.

Another very clear spiritual analogy is that trying to live someone else's life or running in someone else's lane may work at first but eventually a foul smell will be produced. Only when you live out loud what is true to who you are and how you've been uniquely created to be, that a lasting and pleasant fruit is produced.

Many Fires to Put Out

Blood work was done every day, of course, and we would watch for the slightest elevation in white blood cells that would indicate the body's response to a rising threat of infection. His body was doing the best it could to fight, and thank God his lungs and other organs had not been affected. If he had been a smoker, he definitely would have had injured lungs from the smoke inhalation. Thank God, his lungs and body were healthy and strong.

The surgical team removed the donor skin once the body rejected it. Finally, pieces of his own skin were used for transplants in the worst burned areas. On one such occasion, the burn technicians shaved off some skin from his shin area, only to create one of the most difficult wounds ever to recover. Unfortunately, a third-degree burn instead of second-degree was created where the healthy skin had been removed. It seemed to take forever for that new wound to close. So the battle for life continued day after day, week after week, month after month. It was a huge celebration each time a piece of transplanted skin would take and start to grow on his body.

His Handsome Face

Originally, we thought his face was saved from any effects of the fire, but that drastically changed after about a week. His thick, hard beard was growing longer before the skin had time to recover from what at first looked like a sunburn. Doctors were concerned infection would set in, since it was almost impossible to keep his bearded face perfectly clean. As they predicted, the irritated skin became red and filled with pus. The doctors then decided to shave his beard. I was not there at the time of the decision nor when they started shaving, but as I walked into the room I could not believe my eyes! I thought for sure they had lost their minds! *Shaving his beard?*

My first response? "This is total insanity." I made it known, in no uncertain terms, exactly what I thought as I watched the new, sharp razor blade peeling off some of the damaged skin on his face. It was impossible to shave his hard beard without further injury to the existing condition. He begged them to stop, for the pain was intolerable. A nightmare!

I asked them to please not do it again because I had serious questions about the process. I once again received the lecture about the high likelihood of infection that could spread to the rest of his vulnerable body, but again I questioned, "What is the lesser of the two evils—dealing with infection or shaving his skin off his face every day?" That beard was not going to stop growing, so the shaving would not stop either.

When the nurses started shaving him again the next day, I really lost control and demanded they stop shaving him immediately. However, the nurses meticulously followed the doctor's order, which is awesome, except for the fact that the doctor who had written the orders had not yet seen the effect of the first shave. So I stood watch over him until the doctor came to reassess the situation. The shaving orders were stopped. Thank God!

In the days that followed, a big, black, hard scab formed over the whole bearded area of his face. It was quite a mess with the mix of scabs and hair. No one seemed to know how to respond to the way he appeared. From a distance, it looked like he had a big black beard that was, in fact, a hard crust even over his lips. As a result, he was suddenly unable to drink from a glass or a straw. His lips could not latch onto a cup or glass and do what they were supposed to do. So I put a straw in his mouth and pushed it to the corner of his mouth while lightly pressing his lips together. That would be the only way he was able to drink for many days to follow.

What was happening to Hennie's face was such a bizarre occurrence—one the burn team had never seen before, and the doctor thought that infection had already been spreading in that area. The fear that infection was brewing underneath the dark, hard scab would have been devastating had it been true. During the ordered biopsy, I felt as if I could feel the pain when tweezers were used to pull off some of the scabs to send to the lab. All the while, I kept trying to convince the nurse that she had enough samples to culture, but of course, she continued until she had taken enough for the test. Blood was oozing from the places where the scabs had been pulled off his face, and I was angry.

When Hennie and I had a cup of coffee together, I noticed a round dent on his skin in the middle of his cheek. The light hit his face just right to highlight a scar I hadn't noticed before. I looked closely and, sure enough, it was a scar from one of the biopsy spots. Yet another scar serves as a fresh reminder of how painful that must have been, but also how the grace of God beautifully healed so many wounds. Some scars may even go unnoticed, but the important part is that they are completely healed. He has many scars on his body, and I often look at his beautiful, healthy skin with wonder and so much love and adoration, thanking God for the healing and restoration we thought we would never see.

Others Who Didn't Make It

When your body burns to such a degree, the implications plus the possible side effects of the treatment, not to mention the medicine alone, can take out the burn victim. During his hospitalization, I saw several burn patients come into the burn trauma unit who didn't leave alive. I recall a young teenage girl who sustained burns from her head down to her torso. She passed away after a day or two of suffering.

She was a ballerina whose hair somehow caught fire that spread rapidly over the rest of her body. All the hairspray she used to keep her hair up in a bun acted as fuel for the flames. In the shock of the moment, she used the aerosol hairspray to try to put out the flames. Instead of smothering the fire, it accelerated the flames, causing more than half of her body to suffer serious burns. Who would ever have taught a teenage ballerina how to respond in the event her hair caught on fire? Needless to say, her petite young body was unable to withstand the trauma. Her burns were much less severe than Hennie's, but she did not survive.

One day in Hennie's room, I heard an unfamiliar groaning coming from down the hall. By that time, I was part of the furniture in the ward, so I walked over quietly and looked through a door that was slightly ajar. A precious little girl, who must have been around four years old, sat in the scrub tub crying. The sound she made was as if she had grown tired of crying, so she only mustered up repeated sobbing sounds. Her moans were so pitiful they could haunt a person for the rest of his life. I know they haunted me for a long time. Even thinking about this sight and sound is still torturous.

"How did the flames get to this little girl?" "How could this have happened to her?" were some of my cries to God. But tragedy knows no age, gender or race; we are all subject to the brokenness of life on earth. So let's be grateful for skin, for health, for good times. Once again, let's celebrate everything remotely fitting the criteria of goodness. Enjoy the fruit of your labor and toil on earth!

To everything there is a season,
A time for every purpose under heaven:
A time to be born, And a time to die;
A time to plant, And a time to pluck what is planted;
A time to kill, And a time to heal;
A time to break down, And a time to build up;
A time to weep, And a time to laugh;
A time to mourn, And a time to dance;

A time to cast away stones, And a time to gather stones;
A time to embrace, And a time to refrain from embracing;
A time to gain, And a time to lose;
A time to keep, And a time to throw away;
A time to tear, And a time to sew;
A time to keep silence, And a time to speak;
A time to love, And a time to hate;
A time of war, And a time of peace.
(Ecclesiastes 3:1-8)

He has made everything beautiful in its time. Also He has put eternity in their hearts, except that no one can find out the work that God does from beginning to end. I know that nothing is better for them than to rejoice, and to do good in their lives, and also that every man should eat and drink and enjoy the good of all his labor—it is the gift of God. (Ecclesiastes 3:11-13)

Somehow, somewhere, we both had to find the strength to go on. We didn't have much choice. What were my options after all? I was dying on the inside, getting wearier every day, but at least my body was intact. I had to stay strong for Hennie who was not that fortunate.

Once again, the grace to function came only one day, one hour, one minute, one moment at a time. Sometimes, victory is simply dealing with pain one step at a time. The thought of what the future could hold, with no hope of things ever getting better often takes us out of the fight prematurely. This is especially true for those with a desperate need to control the outcome of their lives, or who find comfort in carefully planning the future. Life truly happens where our plans don't pan out, and that is where most of us live—in the detours of life. How often those times turn out to be the main roads after all! To win in life requires flexibility and creativity. Winning in life is redefined many times in any given lifetime.

A Delicate Dance

So what is the wise choice between fighting and pushing to make things happen versus accepting things we didn't expect? This million-dollar question deserves to be pondered for sure. The following are my thoughts:

- There are times to fight
  and times to concede.
- There are times to resist till bloodshed,
  and times to stand back and see where the situation will go.
- There are times to take a stand and be immovable,
  and times to consider the journey and season and flex.
- There are times and issues never ever to give up on,
  and times to live in peace and know God is at work on our behalf.
- There are times to run
  and times to stop.
- There are times to go after your promise and enforce your rights,
  and times to make shine what is already in your hands.
- There are times to be stubborn and feisty,
  and times to shut up and ponder in your heart what God is busy doing on your behalf.
- There are times to take action
  and times to give room.
- There are times to enforce order and discipline,
  and times to create safe places to mess up.
- There are times to take authority and declare how things will go,
  and times to be still and know that He is God.

This is such a delicate dance; with the wrong music, it turns out anything but gracious. The music we need to dance to is God's unique melody for our individual lives. We get distracted so many times when confusion or cares tempt us to stop the song, change the song, or dance to someone else's song. Each one's song is beautiful, with grace that shines when we dance to our own glorious song prepared by God for us. Sometimes we don't like the music or don't know the steps, but if we dance with God, He leads and we follow. Oh, what a grace it is to flow with God, to fight for what is ours, and to know the season for each!

How About You?

Life is not fair, but in the midst of all the pain and uncertainty, God is just. God has a plan for your life. Hell was not made for men and women but as the result of rebellion in heaven that made this world sick.

Satan has been given power here on earth for an appointed time. He is wreaking havoc and working hard to drag to hell with him anyone who will succumb. Make sure you are part of those redeemed by the death and blood of the Lord Jesus Christ! While you are still alive, you can make sure that you won't wake up in hell once you leave this earth.

Hell is real! It's a place of torment and destruction that never ends. The Bible records that hell was created for Satan and his angels who rebelled against God and created not for people. We all have a choice concerning whom and what we follow while we live here on earth—God, through Jesus Christ, or evil, which is contrary to the will and ways of God. Only two eternal kingdoms are in play here on earth—God's kingdom of life and Satan's kingdom of darkness with eternal judgment. In which kingdom are you dwelling?

"The word is near you, in your mouth and in your heart" (that is, the word of faith which we preach): that if you confess with your mouth the Lord Jesus and believe in your heart that God has raised Him from the dead, you will be saved. For with the

heart one believes unto righteousness, and with the mouth confession is made unto salvation. For the Scripture says, "Whoever believes on Him will not be put to shame." For there is no distinction between Jew and Greek, for the same Lord over all is rich to all who call upon Him. For "whoever calls on the name of the Lord shall be saved." (Romans 10:8-13)

Hell and evil are real. Life sometimes hurts. Some consequences remain. Some people will never change. Some outcomes will be painful. But thank God, He is not asleep; He does not slumber. He has compassion on us and is ready to restore us to Himself no matter what is going on in our lives. Not all situations will be restored, but our hearts can always be completely healed if we stay right with God.

May He help us to know the difference while giving us grace to walk in our season and callings—even if it's different from what we had planned.

Prayer

God, I need help. I realize I am lost. I am not sure how I will spend eternity. I believe You sent Jesus to die for me. Today I choose to give You all my heart and all my life. I ask You to redeem my life from the curse of sin and death. Forgive me of all my sin as I forgive those who sinned against me. Lead me not into temptation, but deliver me from evil. From this day forth, I'm a follower of Jesus Christ, and I live to do Your will and learn Your ways. Amen.

6

Where Are You, God?

Staying the Course When the Road Gets Long

T HE NIGHT WAS VERY late. Once again I made sure Hennie was as comfortable as could be expected before I went home. Only a few cars were on the road when I left the hospital in Norfolk to go home to Virginia Beach, where Ma Leen and Yolandie were already fast asleep. As I took the on-ramp to the freeway that night, tears streamed down my face as I talked to God. I had been strong during the day, but the moment I got alone with God, a floodgate of emotions seemingly opened up and spilled out.

My Encounters with God

These talks with God happened quite frequently since the drive home was usually my alone time with God. That night my soul cried out to God as loudly as ever. I told God that no matter what, even if He had turned His back on me, I would not relent but continue to pursue Him with all that was within me. I vividly saw myself holding onto the hem of His garment—not simply touching it like the woman in the Bible, but holding on for dear life like someone clenching a rope while dangling over a very high cliff. I knew with certainty that if I were to let go, I would be gone into the deep abyss of despair, surrounded in cold darkness, wrapped in a heart broken in a million pieces.

I knew God was not turning His back on me, but maybe He was looking away for a moment. At least, that is how it felt. After all, Hennie's condition was not promising, nor was our future, which looked wretchedly hopeless. A bold fighting spirit came over me even in the depths of desolation as I told God once again that I was not going to let

Him go. I was not going to be deterred; rather, I would run as fast as I could to keep up with Him and hold on so tightly that He could not let me go even if He wanted to. In my own strength, I felt utterly lost and alone.

The burden of broken dreams for a future with the man I loved so deeply weighed down heavily on my shoulders.

The husband I once knew was now gone.

Hennie was gone from the life we used to have—lost in his own world of pain, suffering, and confusion. To be honest, I'm not sure exactly where he was in his mind, but I know it was in a place far removed from what we had ever known. He was in what seemed like a bottomless pit that tried to swallow him alive.

Hennie's Encounter with Eternity

On one of those early days, I was sitting in the waiting room, anticipating hearing from the nurse when I could go into Hennie's room. I was never allowed in the scrub area, that "room of torture," which was probably just as well, but I could see him as soon as they had finished dressing his wounds.

The nurse finally appeared and seemed to be in a hurry. "Come quickly," she said. She hurriedly explained that while she was dressing his wounds after the scrubbing in the tub, he had pushed his head back into the airbed and had said, "I think God is calling me home."

She knew what he meant, so she immediately called out his name, asking loudly, "Mr. Becker, what about your wife and little girl in the waiting room?" He opened his eyes as if he had just come back to life. She continued talking to him about his family in order to direct his focus on something good.

I went into the room, loved on him, and reassured him that he was getting so much better. I told him everything was going to be fine in no time. "My love, just hold on a little longer," I begged.

I lied.

I lied to him a lot during that time.

I used to tell him he was getting better when, in fact, he was not. I told him all kinds of things to give him hope during the many gloomy prognoses. I told him how the scrubbing sessions were going to be less frequent and severe and how his skin was growing rapidly as a result of his body's great response to the treatment. "All you have to do is find strength to get through one more day."

"Tomorrow is going to be a better day" became my motto. When it was not better, I told him it was just a small snag in the process of the amazing healing taking place in his body.

Maybe I was not lying after all.

Maybe I was just looking a little further into the future than everyone else. Not much hope existed in the hour, day, or week, so I chose to look several months ahead and even into the next year. I was told that if he should survive, it would take at least two years for him to resume normal activities. I honestly totally disregarded that estimation. I believed it might have been true for others but not for Hennie. I simply knew there was no way we were giving in to the worst-case scenario; a better day was coming—coming sooner than expected!

A Dream Is Future Reality

Pat and Annie Crowder were close friends of ours at the time. Pat was one of Hennie's fellow students at Regent University. One day when Pat came to see Hennie, he talked to me in the waiting room before going in to see his friend. He told me of a dream he had of the future in which Hennie was completely healthy, dressed in street clothing, including short trousers, while our families were having a wonderful time visiting together.

As Pat was talking about the details of his dream, I also started to see the picture in my mind. I saw Hennie sitting in the living room wearing street clothes, enjoying the normal activities of life. God knows that was the furthest thing from his condition at the time, but I saw it. I believed it! Maybe I didn't believe it yet, but I surely chose to hope it. In my mind's eye, the dream was real and a picture in my heart I desperately hoped would come to pass. Some could have said that it was only a dream, but to me it was all I had. A dream was definitely better than the reality that offered mostly dread and despair.

I thank God for people like Pat who loved us and prayed for us. He stormed the throne of God on our behalf and received a prophetic vision. Thank God for all those who stood with us in prayer, believing with great faith for Hennie's healing when humanly speaking it looked impossible. I cannot begin to tell how powerfully that vision stuck with me. It was far-fetched, seemingly impossible, but so much better a picture than what I saw in the natural. Hope! How I thank God for hope. Thank God for those who carry it.

Hope reminds me of an experience we had as a family during a cross-country road trip many years later. We were driving somewhere between Montana and North Dakota in what must have been one of the darkest nights on the planet. Montana is called "Big Sky Country" for a reason. The sky there seems to stretch farther and bigger than the mind can fathom. The road ahead of us into North Dakota was straight and mostly flat, appearing to go on forever. In the far distance we noticed a small, dim light that emerged one moment and was gone the next. It kept happening, causing us to think that we must be seeing a UFO! Not really, but it surely was a fun thought! To us it was the only possible explanation of this strange phenomenon. We were positive that we saw a real light in the distance, but we could not understand why it would disappear repeatedly in such an unexplainable way. We knew we saw a light, but did we? It was clearly present in the far distance, but where did it go?

This phenomenon continued for what could have been an hour or so, until finally the light remained and only grew brighter. We thought if it were a real light, like that of another car driving toward us, surely it would have passed us long ago. But the road was so long and straight that we could see the light of the oncoming car farther than you can imagine. Finally, the car came in full view before our paths crossed. We didn't realize at the time that we were driving the longest stretch of straight road in America, which caused the intermittent appearance of the car's headlights.

What we experienced is an illustration of hope. Hope is that flickering light in the distance that sometimes disappears from plain sight. We knew we saw something, but wondered at times where it went. We then wondered if what we saw was real—even when we knew we saw something! Hope paints a picture in our hearts that faith can hold on to until the fullness of time when it manifests. Hope is the breath of faith, and faith can live no longer than the breath of hope gives life to it. So hold on to hope—even when you feel insecure with doubt looming at your door. Stay focused. Keep expecting God to complete the good work He has started according to His promises for your life. I didn't see God or the answer with my physical eyes during the darkest of times, but with eyes of faith I certainly did. I believed Hennie's healing was real even though it was in the distant future.

Hope is a beautiful intangible, which carried us even when our faith was shaken to the core. Grace, that supernatural ability to get things done and keep on going, accompanied the hope in my heart. The glimmering light of hope kept my head in the heavenlies while grace kept my feet on the ground.

Broken or Bold?

Going though such trauma was about to leave us either very broken or very bold. With that assertion, I was often both of these at the same time, but boldness won at the end. I didn't care if anyone thought I was crazy for I had no time to consider the faithless thoughts of other people. I had a battle on my hands, and I needed to be equipped for the fight.

I got up every day, took a shower, and dressed. Walking around looking like the devil just woke up was never a second thought or an option for me. People frequently commented on how good I looked in the face of what I was going through which, without fail, left me wondering what in the world they meant. If only they could have seen me on the inside, they would have had a different comment for sure. My heart was in shreds, experiencing deep grief and pain—none of which was pretty at all. I often wondered how they expected me to look. Should I have dressed in sackcloth and ashes or in sloppy clothes with ragged, unkempt hair? I instinctively knew I had to maintain good habits that would set me up to fight every day, so the least I could do was to look presentable. Somehow that perspective helped me get a good start to my day. In the worst of circumstances, showing up looking my best was a win for me.

All I knew was to do what I was used to doing, which was to get up, clean up, dress up, and face my day. I'd do my hair the same, my makeup the same, then off I went. Pure grace gave me the strength to keep going in the natural. The unseen supernatural grace of God gave me the power that manifested in the natural, sustaining my testimony and enabling me to keep shining at my point of desperate weakness. Those who could not see God in my circumstances hopefully saw Him in the grace that enabled me to function. I knew without a shadow of a doubt that God was there with me. Hennie and I refused to even consider the alternative. We were not alone in our fight, so we kept going.

What to Call It

Was what happened an accident? People called it an accident, but from the start I had a huge issue with that terminology. An accident supposes something happened by mere happenstance, with heaven and earth being out of control or dozing off for a second. Things sometimes happen accidentally in the sense that we don't mean or plan for them to happen, but then there is God; He is in full control at all times. Was He busy somewhere else at the moment of the accident? Was He looking away, helping someone else, or taking a nap?

Accident—that word was repulsive to me. I vehemently refused to think about what happened to Hennie in that way or to call what happened an accident. In my book, it was an *incident*—not an *accident* at all. His injuries were far too severe and gruesome to even insinuate the incident was accidental or missed by God. Impossible! It was an *accident* in that we didn't plan for it or anticipate it, so I've come to peace with the word in the years to follow.

Defining a Miracle

The God of the universe missed it? If that were the case, He would be a weak, selfish deity in whom I could not believe or trust. God was there. God must have been there. I knew He was there. He witnessed the whole incident. For some reason, He did not save Hennie from getting hurt but allowed him to go through this agony. What happened was an accident in the sense that we didn't expect it or mean for it to happen, but with God, it was no accident. He was in full control.

Many years passed before I went back to God with the question of "Why?" At the time of the intense pain, followed by several years of recovery, I used all of my energy to maintain a close relationship with God. My focus was to overcome each obstacle that stood between Hennie and his complete restoration. No time or energy was at my disposal for asking questions, but only to overcome.

A month or so into this ordeal, I received a phone call from a video producer at the 700 Club who was interested in filming our story. The 700 Club is an international television ministry connected to Regent University where Hennie was a student. They were interested in telling about Hennie's survival and how anyone could still be alive after such a fiery experience. God saved his life indeed, which was something totally worth telling, but not far into our conversation I could clearly see that they were looking for a story of instant victory and miracles. They wanted something they could edit into a three-minute clip of how he burned up one day and woke up healed the next.

Maybe a little exaggeration on my part, yes, but remember, I was in war mode. I was probably not in the best emotional state to build someone else's faith while being in the midst of a life-threatening situation with more questions than answers. I tried to explain that although God had already performed many outrageous miracles, we were not yet out of the woods. Hennie could still have died any day. We were still walking out our miracle that this time turned out to be for the long haul—a marathon—as opposed to a sprint to the finish line. Oftentimes the greatest miracles play out over time, yet all of us would prefer them to manifest overnight.

The truth is, the message wasn't exactly what anyone wanted to hear—not even me. The best story is one with a clear beginning followed by a great ending of living happily ever after. The problem with Hennie's story was that the time between the flames and the healing did not yet hold a story. But that is exactly where the whole story transpired; back then we were walking in lonely darkness, yet in complete grace accompanied by the power of God's presence.

Why is it that we cannot believe in miracles without seeing the desired happy ending? Why are miracles defined by the endings rather than the times in the valley of the shadow of death where the real battles are won? Thank God for the times we do experience great endings, yet most often that is not the case. You and I are not defined by our tragedies or their endings; rather, we are defined by how we walk them out. If we were defined by our tragedy, how would you explain

Stephen along with the many who suffered according to Hebrews 11? They are mentioned at the end of the chapter. It's very comfortable to read Hebrews 11 only up to the middle of verse 35; then suddenly the theme turns and becomes quite distressing and even painful. The eleventh chapter of Hebrews, the faith chapter, continues: *"Still others had trial of mockings and scourgings, yes, and of chains and imprisonment"* (Hebrews 11:36).

I often refer to verse 36 as the "still others" verse. When is the last time we've considered the "still others" of the Hall of Faith in Hebrews chapter 11? Those are the true heroes of faith with extraordinary lives who never saw that for which they believed but continued in faith till the end. Those were the ones who gruesomely died for their faith. As a matter of fact, many of our fathers of faith never saw the complete manifestation of what they believed for—only in part.

Try to find the "logic" in verse 39 that states that these have obtained a good testimony even though never obtaining the promise. Miracles sometimes have the Hallmark movie endings to which we are so addicted, but other times they are far removed from this earth with endings in God's presence. Sometimes our miracles are even greater when the endings or rewards are in heaven instead of on earth.

Don't ever settle for defeat when you can't see the fulfillment of what you believe. Some days God's grace on your life with His power in your step is as miraculous as it gets. Don't listen to those who judge only according to what they can see, but remember that every step or stand you take in the power of God when you go through pain is your miracle!

When Faith Is the Miracle

Where was God when my grandmother was dying after the birth of my mom? My grandfather was a man of faith. Oupa Albert Marais was a beloved pastor, greatly respected by his family and others. He believed in God alone to save his wife when she was in desperate need of a miracle in order to stay alive. Those were crazy days of radical faith!

As a young man, in the early 1920s, my grandfather got saved to a life of blind, uncompromising faith in the powerful providence of God through Jesus Christ. When my mom was born, the placenta remained inside her mother's body despite the midwife's endeavors to save the situation. My grandfather went to prayer. On his knees, he gave his wife into God's hands, resolving to live with the consequences of his profound faith in Jesus Christ. The Scriptures were his teacher, so he believed for a miracle according to the promises of God.

She died. Where was God? Why did Grandpa not call a doctor? Could anything have been done to help her—even in those days of limited medical advances? Those were questions I carried with anger in my heart because my mom never got to experience the loving arms of the one who gave her birth. How cruel and selfish! But who am I to judge? Only God can judge correctly.

Many years ago, God graciously brought me to a place of healing in this matter. I admitted my anger, forgave, and received forgiveness, which brought the peace in my heart I needed. My grandfather was one of those "still others," so today I admire him for his firm, uncompromising faith in God. He obviously knew something I didn't. Maybe there were no medical solutions, or maybe his faith in God was without wavering even till death. Those years, in many circles of faith, they did what was referred to as "praying through." People would pray nonstop even through the night, until they saw a miracle or God answering in some way or another. Sometimes it meant praying until healing or death came.

I thank God this was not the case with me when as a four-year-old I suffered severely with chronic bronchitis, which oftentimes left me gasping for air as I struggled to breathe. I remember how my mom boiled Vicks in a pot of water on a Primus stove right next to my bed. The Vicks steam opened my airways so I could breathe easier. I can still see Oupa Marais on his knees at the end of my bed, interceding for me for what seemed like hours at a time. Heaven touched earth during those times. God answered his faith-filled, tenacious prayers for my complete healing. I know today that losing his wife did not deter him from trusting God—no matter the circumstance, no matter what people said, no matter the temporary earthly outcome.

We have so many precious memories of those who have gone before us. They preached the gospel, believed God for the impossible, led people to Christ, and persevered despite hardships as long as they could lead one more soul to Jesus. They lived not to gather earthly stuff, but rather to gather the harvest for God's kingdom. Grandpa was the same man who regularly preached the gospel of Jesus on the open field or in the middle of the main street in his town. All he needed was someone with an instrument who could sing in order to attract an audience to whom he could preach. Before long, people knelt in the dirt as they tearfully accepted Jesus Christ as their personal Savior.

My mom told me how he would not wait but baptized those same people the very next day. I love that heaven-focused determination! He didn't wait for people to show up at his church; rather, he radically pursued the lost any way he saw fit. This outlook stemmed from the same unwavering faith he had in God to see his wife healed—no questions, no bitterness, no giving up—just onward Christian soldier! Yes, those were different days.

What a reunion awaits us in heaven when the circle of the family will be unbroken! We will all be together for the first time—even with those who still have to make a decision to follow Christ. May God have great mercy that will draw them close before it's too late!

Oftentimes when I get in my fancy SUV to drive to church, I think about how Grandpa visited his congregants on a bicycle. He didn't receive a salary from the church for many years after entering full-time ministry, but somehow he managed to feed his family. I then realize how he paid a price for many things he never saw in this life. His reward in heaven must be grand, but I just know my big house and nice SUV are part of his fruit here on earth, and I'm incredibly humbled! He bought a car in later years, but he didn't count it loss to get on his bicycle to go pray for someone when that was all he had. These saints are in the company of the "still others" along with those dying for the sake of Jesus Christ every day in our world. There is too much we don't understand to cast judgment or lose faith. As long as there is life, any time is too soon to judge or stop believing God! He has the last say.

Working His Way Back to a New Normal

Where was God during those cursed moments of Hennie's rehabilitation on days too hard to recount? Where was God? As the skin started to grow back, it was as stiff as a board, yet extremely fragile. Scar tissue grew back but without elasticity and often void of certain skin structures such as hair follicles and sweat glands. It also grew in a bumpy, unruly, clustery form as it seemed to have lost the DNA code of how it was before the injury. I call these skin contractures "crazy growth" because the body knows it must grow skin in spite of seemingly losing the blueprint to go by. On the other hand, his second-degree burned skin mostly grew back in perfect shape as it was before the burn.

The scar tissue eventually became stronger than the normal tissue, yet was still unable to stretch. Without the intervention of tight body suits that controlled the crazy growth, he would have been left with bulges of thick skin-like tissue unable to bend or move. In the recovery of burn patients in developing nations void of proper medical care, people suffering greatly for the rest of their lives, as a result of skin contractures, are often seen.

Hennie suffered burns in many areas that had to stretch in order to regain normal use, such as under his arms, the top of his hands and fingers, elbows, etc. Those areas had to be forced to stretch during the healing process, which caused excruciating pain. Early in the process of rehabilitation while he was still in the trauma unit, the therapists started coming to his bed to bend and maneuver his body to prevent its losing flexibility and, therefore, losing use.

The therapy consisted of bending and rotating his arms, legs, and other joints by pushing them into full-motion positions. The therapy became yet another torturous appointment on the daily schedule. As they pushed back his arms to stretch the new skin in areas such as the armpit, the skin cracked and broke open with blood pouring out all over the sheets. The broken skin had 24 hours to start healing until the next session when it was pushed, pulled, stretched, and left bleeding once again.

The therapy was necessary; otherwise, he would end up with skin everywhere but with his limbs frozen in place. He had to keep his fists closed to stretch the skin on top of his hands even when he went to sleep. For many months, and even years post-burn, he had to force his fists to close every morning after they had relaxed in his sleep. For the longest time, this was the first ritual each morning even before he got out of bed. This simple exercise pulled the skin on the top of his hands so scar tissue did not set his hands in an open position. In doing so, the new skin often tore and cracked open, bleeding over and over again until the stretching no longer caused trauma.

He also had to wear tight custom-made body suits called JOBST that exerted constant pressure on the scar tissue to prevent contractures—the out-of-control crazy growth. The suits were full body suits from his neck down to his fingers, all the way to his ankles. For about a year, I had to help him get into a tight skin suit in the morning, then at night help him out of it so he could take a shower and get a break from the discomfort, only to get back into it before going to bed. Getting these suits changed every day caused new skin to tear and bleed for many months during recovery. For many months after he came home, putting on and taking off the JOBST was part of his daily routine.

Wearing these suits was a total nuisance to say the least, but obeying the doctor and faithfully wearing them paid off in the end. Hennie regained full motion in all his joints without bulges or deep ridges of debilitating scar tissue. The recovery of scar tissue in and of itself is a magnificent miracle that leaves us still in awe today. I think back and seriously do not know how we got through those times, but we did. Wild days, but God was there!

After more than a month in the hospital, the medical authorities decided that he had to start the therapy of learning how to walk again. He had completely lost all muscle tone in his entire body which left him unable to do the most basic of movements, such as lifting food to his mouth to eat. His hands limply gripped food or utensils but shook so much that he lost the food before he could lift it to his mouth. He was unable to lift a book or stand on his own. His whole body shook when he tried to stand, and his head bobbed because he had trouble keeping it upright. His whole body was so gaunt that he looked like a bag of bones, with his once swollen face appearing starkly cavernous. But he was alive, thank God!

In the gym, the therapist wrapped leather belts around his body to hold him up so he could start walking. They pulled him to his feet by the straps between two bars so he could hold on and walk. I found myself standing in front of him, cheering him on to take that first step as if he were a baby learning how to walk for the first time. His legs were too heavy for him to lift up to put one foot in front of the other, so we helped him lift his feet so he could try to take a step.

Taking steps was even more awkward because he now had "foot drop" as a result of nerve damage caused by the stents that were placed under his legs while he was still bedridden. The stents were strapped underneath his legs to keep them straight so the scar tissue would not tighten and "freeze" his legs in the bent position. I know, never a dull moment!

The picture of Hennie standing between those two bars trying to hold on with the therapist holding him in a standing position by the straps around his body and his looking at me with eyes that said, "I'm trying really hard, but my body won't work," is forever etched in my brain.

As far as mobility is concerned, when the entire body suffers trauma, what is not used is lost. The old idiom *Use it or lose it* is true. No matter how strong you are, if you don't use it, it's not staying. The muscles were there, the potential was inside of him to recover what he once had, but it took another fierce battle, as well as an abundance of work, to regain what he had lost. The battle was all worth it because he was alive, and God was with us every moment of every day.

How About You?

It is never a good time to give up since you have access to the Creator of the universe, who is always with you. God wants to see you succeed in life. Success is redefined several times in a lifetime. When things get tough, we may have to embrace new truths. Take a moment to be honest with yourself. Allow God to open up those areas where new light needs to shine in order for you to feel the warmth of hope again.

The following two truths will serve you well if you sincerely take hold of them:

1] **The real story and testimony of your life happens in between the beginning and end of life events.**

- ◆ We live in the journey—not the beginning or the end of a matter. The beginning and end come and go, but it's during the journey that we have to deal with what happens. That is where we need to stay strong in what we are called to do.

◆ We are also not defined by what comes into our life but how we respond, what we do with it, and how it affects our next season.

◆ Some seasons are short and mild; others are long and dreary where it may be a while before the tide turns. We may weather a painful event, but during a long journey we are likely to grow weary and lose hope.

◆ Focusing only on the way out of a season leads to giving up—on God, on hope—living a miserable life. God is with you. The season will end.

◆ Live in your miracle every day. As that alone sometimes requires an act of God, it is where you'll experience the greatest power of God in your life and get to know God deeply.

2] **Several vital structures in your life will hold you up in the times when you feel you're falling.** Overarching everything is the power and grace of God, but that is evident in many forms when life events strip away the frills and fancies of this world. Here are seven other key structures that come into play to sustain you:

◆ **God's Word**
The Bible brings true life, cuts through any force of darkness, and holds every promise that is ours through the blood of Jesus Christ that paid for it all. We can rely on no greater power because once God speaks, no word falls to the ground or returns void. The same words that spoke the world into existence still hold it up today. Planets stay in place, and oceans roar within their boundaries. What was

spoken in the beginning of time is still in full effect. God does not have to wake up each day to reset the cosmos. His words never lose their effect, power, or life. Neither do the promises of God. They are spoken, yet now it is up to us to line up with them to reap the life they bring.

♦ **Faith-People**
These people of faith are crucial in life, especially when our own faith and hope wane; it happens to us all from time to time. The will of God is that we do not do life alone. Our responsibility is to surround ourselves with faith-people—those who will stand in faith with us even when all others grow weary on the journey.

♦ **Love-People**
These individuals are the ones in our lives who love us un-conditionally and truly want to see us prosper. We can be fooled by superficial love declarations, but this love goes deeper than the mere sound of words. You'll know them by the way they sincerely want the best for your life. They will stand with you in faith for your miracle, defend you in your absence, and selflessly believe in your dreams—never to judge harshly but love unconditionally.

♦ **Good Habits**
Not letting go of habits that remind you of goodness will help you maintain a sense of normalcy when nothing else seems normal—whether it is your morning coffee ritual, celebrating birthdays, preparing a feast for the holidays, go-ing to church, Friday night friend hangouts, making your bed every morning, or washing your car every week. Such beauty and strength exists in good habits. If you don't have any, take heart; it's never too late to start making some.

Good habits will serve you well in all times, especially during the down times.

♦ **Examples**

Examples worth following will offer viable options when you feel lost in a gloomy night. Who are the people whose testimonies and examples speak of the power and mercy of God in your life? Treasure those! Remember the positive outcome of their faith when you are in need of the same. God is not a respecter of persons. What He has done for others, He will surely do for you also.

♦ **Steady Feet**

They are imperative in times of turmoil. Move slowly. Don't make any harsh or impulsive decisions. Wait before you judge or say something prematurely. When many things around you are changing or you're wrapped up in sudden trials, don't be tempted or fall under pressure to make rash decisions. Decisions, especially important ones, are best executed after the dust settles. At times you may have to think on your feet and make a fast call, but for the most part, be cautious in the dark when you know where you are but are uncertain of what lies ahead.

♦ **Drama-Free Zone**

Avoid drama at all costs. Drama unfolds when you react instead of respond to a situation. Allowing drama to envelop you may land you in a worst-case scenario which, in turn, will zap the precious emotional energy you need to stay on top of things instead of beneath them. Cut the drama! Don't become part of the storm; rather, step aside to become part of the will of God in the situation. Having a propensity for drama may present a challenge. Be mindful of it though. You will get stronger as you stretch in self-control.

Can anything ever separate us from Christ's love? Does it mean he no longer loves us if we have trouble or calamity, or are persecuted, or hungry, or destitute, or in danger, or threatened with death?...And I am convinced that nothing can ever separate us from God's love. Neither death nor life, neither angels nor demons, neither our fears for today nor our worries about tomorrow—not even the powers of hell can separate us from God's love. No power in the sky above or in the earth below—indeed, nothing in all creation will ever be able to separate us from the love of God that is revealed in Christ Jesus our Lord.

(Romans 8:35, 38-39 NLT)

7

God Is Still Close

Holding on When Faith Runs Low

WE DID NOT HAVE medical insurance when we came to America because our student budget was quite tight. We were young, healthy, filled with faith to follow our dreams, challenged only by the call of God on our lives. As long as we had assurance and we were in the will of God, nothing was too hard or asking too much. Not one thought was given to the possibility of disaster's coming near us—how wonderfully innocent youth is! Ignorant, yes, yet wonderful.

Making It Work

I worked from my home as a hairdresser for extra income while Hennie worked in the media center at the university. As an international student, he was allowed to work only thirteen hours a week on campus at minimum wage. Having that income was great, although it was not enough to provide for all we needed; therefore, I was happy to do my part. Even with both of our incomes, we still needed God's intervention to make ends meet, which was always the case.

For us to have been able to come to the United States in the first place was miraculous since it was expensive, seemingly out of reach, and a difficult decision to present to all of our family in the homeland. As legal immigrants, we were not eligible for a credit card, a bank loan, or debt of any kind. We only had what was in our checking account, and as a result, we lived on the edge for the most part. We had no problem with that at all, as we anticipated that surviving in America would not be a walk in the park. Since it was the land of opportunity, we were determined to make it work.

We were happy. How could we have asked for more? We had a place to call home, food, a car, and money for gas. The sky was the limit as far as our expectations and dreams were concerned. Looking back, we really were wealthy because we had zero debt! To be young, healthy and full of faith is beautiful.

As long as I was surrounded by people with hair, I knew I could earn money. Regent was such a place. Little handwritten advertisements with my phone number on a couple of the student bulletin boards on campus attracted an abundance of business. I kept as busy as I wanted to be since I could control my own schedule. My job was perfect for the season we were in because Yolandie was home with me even while I worked. Due to the circumstances, we adjusted to the new culture and strange world together. Hennie had long days at school, so Yolandie was my little play buddy during down times when I had no clients. We did her hair, played dress up, read books, and learned the ABC's, which helped Yolandie thrive even in the absence of other friends and family.

Beautiful New Culture and Friends

It turned out that doing hair was a perfect way to meet potential friends in a strange country. We met people from all over the country and the world, many of whom became dear friends for many years to follow. They had a stylist with an accent; I had business. They had affordable hair care; we had an income. We all had new friends; it was a win-win situation for all.

This is how my business grew: first, the male students called to get haircuts before their wives made appointments for the rest of the family. It soon dawned on me that the women first sent their husbands for haircuts so they could judge my skills before trusting me with their own hair. I didn't blame them at all! Hair days became bonding times and opportunities to experience the new culture for Yolandie and me.

I felt like I was being schooled in American culture with more surprises than I could possibly anticipate. I didn't need long to realize that English and American were two different languages! Although English is my second language, I thought I knew it fairly well. However, some people had accents that I simply could not understand! Even with intense listening on my part, I faced a twofold challenge—a second language as well as a strange accent. For the life of me, no matter how hard I tried, I could not understand some folks, especially those from the South, where no distinction was made in the pronunciation of words such as counseling and canceling. And with the New Yorkers…it took me forever to figure out that "cu-aw-fee" was coffee! Very confusing for a green Afrikaans-speaking girl as well as the source of many great laughs!

A Very Different Friday

Hennie's accident happened on a Friday around noon, right after I got home from being part of the audience during the live broadcast of the 700 Club, which had featured Reinhard Bonnke as the guest. I'd known him from his prolific and dynamic ministry in South Africa, especially in my hometown of Cape Town. His role as the commencement speaker at Hennie's graduation from seminary in Johannesburg, South Africa, held sentimental memories for us. I did not know him personally though he was very well-known in South Africa as a hero of faith, a man used by God in performing astounding miracles. Even the dead have been raised under his ministry—not to mention the lame who walked, the blind who saw, and the souls who were saved from hell. He touched the lives of millions of people in Africa as he ministered to huge crowds in many nations.

The student body at Regent University had chapel meetings every Friday at noon. During one of those meetings, one of our student friends received word about Hennie's incident. Immediately, the students and the faculty rallied in prayer for Hennie's survival. Another one of the attendees was a Regent employee who worked with student services, which handled health insurance issues. She immediately checked to see if we had medical insurance coverage, which was compulsory for all students enrolling for the semester that began that month. As it turned out our medical insurance had become effective only one day before the accident! We all were stunned and relieved to say the least. By God's great mercy, He provided.

We could never have imagined incurring medical bills amounting to hundreds of thousands of dollars after three months in the hospital with a significant amount of time spent in the intensive care unit as well as undergoing many procedures and surgeries. Thank God, we had insurance that covered 80 percent of all our bills. The remaining 20 percent still exceeded $250,000. The same God who created us, whose voice we followed to a far land, who gave us financial coverage for this tragedy, who was surely able to save us from the whole thing to begin with, had a plan. Why He allowed Hennie to be burned remains His business, yet leaves us in awe of how He cares about all the details of our lives—especially our trials. How can we be silent while we are so incredibly grateful to still have voices to speak of His love that saved us?

One of the Regent students served as Reinhard Bonnke's driver while he was a guest of the university. On their way to the airport, the student asked Mr. Bonnke if he would mind stopping at the hospital to pray for Hennie, which of course, he agreed to do. They both laid hands on Hennie's body while agreeing in faith for complete restoration. To this day Hennie has no recollection of that prayer time, but I was greatly encouraged by their prayer of faith. I knew that more faith being exercised by more people would be more effective in my husband's restoration. How amazing was it for this great man of faith to be in the right place at the right time to stand with us for a miracle? In the darkest of nights God always shines His light, making all the difference. Even when it's hard for us to see or believe, God is there!

A Very Different Spirit

Witnessing the response of the students as they stood together to form an army for the fight ahead was quite incredible. At that same Friday chapel meeting, they also received an offering for us—the first of many to follow. No one understands a student living on faith and fumes better than another one who does the same; therefore, the response was profound. They had a spirit of love and generosity that was very different from anything I'd ever witnessed in my lifetime, even among believers. The incredible support meant the world to us. We never felt abandoned or alone, not even for a minute. Remarkable, especially as we were strangers in a foreign land, far from our loved ones and family.

Throughout this tumultuous journey, we received money from many sources to cover our daily needs; God took care of us up to the last detail. Our church, our friends, the families of our friends, other churches, and even strangers supported us generously. Dr. Horner managed our bills initially, so I'm not even sure how much was given, but I know our expenses were covered. Despite everything, we didn't lose the house. Furthermore, our rent and all our living expenses were met. We never ceased to be amazed at how people gave without expecting anything in return.

Even the faculty meeting at the university included a collection for us. We never asked for anything during the whole ordeal; nonetheless, the mercy of God through the generosity of the people was unbelievable. Even after Hennie came home, we received countless notes, prayers, and checks in the mail from people in widespread places.

What kind of people are they, these Americans? Generous to the core they are, relentlessly believing in a better future for all. This is truly a big-hearted nation that takes care of her own as well as the foreigners in her midst. Never in my wildest dreams had I ever thought I'd be called an alien, but I was. Thank God we were in a place with the most special group of people in the universe! They took us in, loved us, and carried our dreams when we were weak, until we could recover. While every rule has an exception, we have experienced the hearts of enough Americans to know they are intrinsically generous. This is how I will forever remember the beauty of how they rally around the injured and disadvantaged. Such generosity is certainly not the case in most parts of the world!

Debt Threatened to Destroy Us

We still had several hundreds of thousands of dollars in medical debt, with no idea how to pay it. Hennie's hospital stay was quite extensive, so the bills started arriving long before he was discharged. I went to the accounting office in the hospital to gather the details of the bills, as well as to figure out how to pay for them. The representative was starkly impersonal, clearly following all of the red tape of a large organization. Suddenly, I was plunged into yet another battle of gigantic proportions. I understood she was merely doing her job, but I quickly realized that there was little room for compassion and negotiation when it came to money. We had to pay our debt. I was not opposed to that obligation, yet realized there had to be additional options besides rolling over and dying—that is, dying financially. The least I could do was explore possible doors to favor according to James 4:2, that says, *"You do have not because you do not ask."*

At first, I was very intimidated. The astronomical debt was owed to a corporation with great legal power that had rendered life-saving medical care for Hennie. I wanted to back off and just do exactly as I was told. The idiom *warm and fuzzy* didn't exist in those medical offices, so I decided to go along with another idiom: *Business is busi-*

ness. I may have looked like a scared little woman from Africa whose husband was dying in the burn ward, except for the fact that inside me lived the Creator of the universe. I was going to have my say.

Jesus said in Matthew 10:16 that we are to be wise as serpents and harmless as doves. Well, this was my test. I wanted the best care for Hennie, while at the same time I also wanted to negotiate the bills. My skills were no match for the gigantic debt that was looming over us. I knew it would take an act of God for it to change or for us to be able to pay; however, I was still the one who had to push back on earth and lean into heaven for a miracle. God was the star of the show, while I kept putting one foot in front of the other.

My reasoning was that the hospital was doing well collecting 80 percent of the debt. If a margin of expected loss existed on their end, I wanted to benefit from it. Logical, right? Well, that's what I thought. Therefore, I reminded the accounts receivable clerk that the hospital was doing well collecting 80 percent of our bills and that we were conscientious foreigners who had made adequate provision for medical coverage. The medical insurance hadn't been our idea but God's because He is my Dad. I asked her to communicate my request to those who made the final decision to accept a portion of the remaining 20 percent as we were students with no available income to cover all of it.

She looked at the wedding ring on my finger while suggesting we find possessions of value to sell, such as diamonds, furs or any other items that might help us cover the bills. *What was she thinking? That I owned a farm in Africa?* I did have a fairly decent diamond on my finger, but it alone would only have been enough for probably one day's rate in the intensive care unit—a mere drop in the hospital debt bucket. She also mentioned that they had long-term payment plans available, much like a home mortgage, which they would be more than happy to set up for us. Our indebtedness was equal to the cost of a very nice house at that time. Just the mere thought of that debt made my heart sink.

First of all, I was crushed by the thought of selling my ring. No. It's just a ring, but enough is enough! Secondly, the thought of needing a lifetime to pay off that debt nauseated me. I left it at that and decided to wait for the next bill to see if it would show a different balance. After all, it would be years before we would have money to start paying off a lifetime debt. Even if we decided to give up on our dreams and go back to South Africa, the debt would have doubled in South African currency. I could see no way out and no viable answer on how to pay these bills. Not yet. At least not that we knew of at the time.

Months later we received a phone call from the hospital informing us of their decision to accept the 80-percent insurance coverage. We owed them nothing! All the bills were included—hospital, doctors, therapy, etc. God had worked on our behalf behind the scenes. The relief was great, to say the least, with such a huge financial burden lifted from our shoulders—a miracle that changed our lives. Some people suggested they probably compromised because we had grounds for claims of negligent practices that had caused Hennie additional suffering, surgeries, and treatments. Taking such an action had never been an option to us—a horse we chose not to saddle. Filing a suit would have been horrible seed in the ground; instead, we chose God as our provider. That settled it for us, and we knew God was with us.

He Didn't Die!

Hennie stayed in the game of survival by the power of God, together with the host of believers who cheered him on. Every day was a miracle. Great was the celebration when he was finally able to leave the burn trauma unit for continued care in the step-down area. We planned for his discharge from the hospital as soon as he could walk, eat by himself, and his blood work was normal. He still had many open wounds, but by that time I was a pro at taking care of him. We witnessed his getting stronger little by little every day. Thank God for hospitals, and even more for the day you leave. That was always the goal, to get out of there as soon as possible, for that meant he was closer to returning to normal.

We wanted to be home before Thanksgiving, and all of us, including the whole medical team, were ready to see him go home as soon as possible. We were all extremely proud of his progress, fully convinced all the pain and push to get well were over. At least, almost over! He was finally able to sit up much more, eat by himself, and even walk short distances on his own. I noticed that he was bent over when he walked, although I didn't give it much thought at the time. The focus was on going home as soon as the results on a final battery of blood tests sealed the deal. The big day came. Ma Leen and Yolandie had the house ready, including of course, his favorite meal and dessert on the table set with the finest ware we owned. Did I mention she was one fantastic cook?

Wait, bent over? Why was he bent over when he walked? Why was he not able to walk up straight? I had thought his body was stiff from the skin transplants. But then one of the doctors who saw him in the hallway that morning halted the discharge procedures in order to investigate the cause of the problem.

I thought Hennie was fine. All I could do was pace the hallways to calm the irritation of the delay. While the doctor was still in the room with Hennie, the latest blood work results came back, indicating elevated white blood cells. No! Not white blood cells! Those were the little soldiers in the blood which meant that a war was still going on somewhere in his body! More blood work, more time. Noon became 3:00 p.m., 3:00 p.m. became 6:00 p.m., 6:00 p.m. became another night in the hospital, more x-rays, until the culprit could be arrested. This culprit was the one that caused him to walk bent over; the one that loomed out of sight, hiding somewhere in his abdomen; and the cursed reason for the white blood cells fighting, relentlessly tormenting Hennie's body, unwilling to let go or give up the fight!

Not Yet

The delicious festivities that had been prepared for Hennie's home-coming the night before turned into leftovers void of any fanfare. Back in the hospital room the next morning, I sat alone waiting for him to return from imaging. I cried out to God from a place of absolute weariness in the fight. I was tired of this ordeal, tired of fighting, even tired of praying the same prayers over and over. As I sat next to the empty bed, all I knew to do was grab my Bible to feverishly find some sense of calm. I experienced the powerful presence of God with me, yet I had become convinced He was tired of all my prayers—the same prayers. *Here we go again, God* was my sigh. *I've been praying what seemed like the same prayers for such a long time, over and over, day after day!*

God must have been tired of all my prayers. I was. On top of that, maybe my repetitive prayers were signs of disbelief and, therefore, not pleasing to God. Maybe I had to thank God for healing instead of praying so much. I had heard preachers say it was a sign of unbelief to ask the same requests repeatedly in prayer. We should just stay in faith while expecting the miracle any moment because God had already answered when we prayed.

Well, I did that. I was quite desperate. I found myself praying repetitive prayers, wondering if I was out of faith or disappointing God. I often begged God to forgive me where I failed, in case my prayers were not acceptable to Him.

I opened my daily devotional, and God started speaking to me so tenderly with the grace, acceptance and comfort only found in His presence. I read where Jesus was praying in the garden the night in which He was betrayed.

He went a little farther and fell on His face, and prayed saying, "O My Father, if it is possible, let this cup pass from Me; nevertheless, not as I will, but as You will." (Matthew 26:39)

Again, a second time, He went away and prayed, saying, "O My father, if this cup cannot pass away from Me unless I drink it, Your will be done." (Matthew 26:42)

So He left them, went away again, and prayed the third time, saying the same words. (Matthew 26:44)

Three times!
Jesus prayed the same prayer three times?
This passage was my moment of freedom!

How foolish can we be! God never gets tired of us or of our heartfelt, honest, and sincere prayers. He is our Father, acquainted with our weakness, ready to come to our rescue when we call on Him.

So, Onward!

If the Son of God in His fleshly suffering prayed three times for the same thing, surely it's acceptable for me to pray the same words three hundred times. So onward, Christian soldier! Onward I went; onward I prayed the same prayer as I had many times before. I believed those test results were going to come back negative. They didn't. I believed his body was healed. It wasn't. I believed Hennie was going home on a specific day. He didn't. I had more to deal with than the number of times God would allow me to pray the same prayer. Oh, but for the beauty of the Father's merciful and loving heart!

The doctor made a drawing on a piece of paper to explain to us what was going on in Hennie's body. A mass had appeared in his chest area, but where it was located was still unclear. The options he gave us of where it could be located, pending further testing, included in his lung, liver, or intestinal area. *Okay, wow! What a choice!*

My response? "Let's pick the least serious one."

Even with further testing, the medical team found it hard for some reason to know exactly what was going on, so they scheduled exploratory surgery. Their best educated guess was that the mass was in or on the liver.

O God, no! Not again. This is not happening!

Emergency surgery was scheduled that same Sunday night. I went to my friend's house near the hospital to have dinner and to be close by to go see Hennie after surgery. Dr. Nuss was invited to observe the surgery and was able to give me the first update when he joined us later for dinner. The problem involved Hennie's gallbladder. He had developed an empyema of the gall bladder, which meant that his gallbladder was filled with pus. The infection had spread through the wall of the gallbladder into the adjacent organs which were all firmly attached to each other. The surgeon could not tell where the organ began or ended as the whole area was one big inflammatory mass. The best that could be done at this point was to insert large suction drains into the gallbladder, which came out through the partly open incision.

The incision had, of course, been made through the healed burn wound, so Hennie now faced the danger of infection spreading to the entire burn surface. There was now direct contact between the skin and the infected gallbladder. The surgeons were not able to remove the gallbladder, for they had no way of knowing where to cut or what to take out. His chest cavity was literally one infected, inflamed mess. This same diagnosis, pronounced ten years earlier with the more limited medical technology available at that time, would have been fatal.

When I walked into Hennie's room after surgery that night, I was shaken by what I saw. Once again he was confined to that despised hospital bed, and he was groaning in pain with tubes protruding from his body. A huge incision from the sternum around the rib cage all the way to the side of his chest left a gaping wound packed with gauze with rubber tubing extending through the wound. Adjacent to the wound was another opening where an even bigger rubber tube had been inserted to drain the pus from the infected area into a bag next to the bed. This tube was also connected to a pump of sorts that rhythmically and gently sucked the pus from inside his body.

The sound of that machine was like Satan himself mocking me. I hated it! I could hear the sound all the way down the hallway when I arrived or left his room. To me, it was like the sound of evil I'll never forget. I was upset. I was so angry. I was also very helpless. Hennie didn't acknowledge me in the room either. All he could do was groan from the intense post-surgery pain.

My head was spinning. *How could we have come this far now to see him die? And the pain—isn't enough enough?* This ordeal was now officially more than I could handle—way more. I was not trying to be difficult. I simply could not bear it any longer. I shook myself, gathered any shreds of hope I could find, and decided to just get through the night. That was all I could muster up—just get through one more night!

God alone knew what Hennie was experiencing. He was the one in pain who had to survive. I sat with him and stroked his face and arms all through that night. I didn't leave his side because he seemed fragile, as if one wrong move could be his last. The nurses had their hands full with all of the other patients for whom they had to provide care. I was not leaving.

I learned quickly how to take care of him with the added paraphernalia attached to his body. The bag had to be emptied, yellow draining discharge measured, and new wounds dressed. The goal was to keep the wound draining. If it stopped expelling pus, serious complications would have resulted with the gunk staying inside his body. Needless to say, I prayed for every bit of pus to leave his body in not the most gracious of terms. That feeling of absolute anger over his condition was the state of my mind—the passion kept me from completely falling apart.

A Bug in His Blood

It took a couple of days for Hennie to get somewhat comfortable and out of the excruciating pain. Cultures revealed staphylococci bacteria in his bloodstream. This so-called "hospital bug" had roamed his body before settling in his gallbladder. I immediately knew when it happened, but casting blame was not going to heal my husband.

Back in the burn trauma unit, I constantly kept watch over the IV needle sites on Hennie's body to alert the nurses in the event that a needle slipped into the tissue instead of remaining in the vein. An IV needle in the tissue caused the area to become inflamed and prevented the medicine from getting into the veins where it was supposed to go. The needles then had to be replaced, which was uncomfortable for the most part, especially when the technicians had trouble inserting the needle perfectly into the vein. The more frequently the veins had to be punctured, the more problematic finding good veins for the IV needles became. Finding a vein under normal circumstances is difficult enough, but when both arms and legs have suffered third-degree fire burns, no veins are readily available. The IV has to be inserted through burned tissue. And of course, the veins that are being used last only so long before they become inflamed and blocked. After several months of IVs, there were simply no veins left.

One night the tech tried multiple times to find a vein before the IV was finally successfully placed on top of his foot. Finding that vein was quite a struggle, as well as exhausting for both patient and technician. For some reason, the technician was not wearing gloves, which was odd at the time, but in the throes of the battle, I dismissed it. I did not feel it was my place to say anything, especially since these episodes of finding veins could get quite hectic. The medicine had to be delivered into the veins to fight the infection that could be potentially fatal, while at times the veins were simply not to be found.

I do have a tendency to see and note details, which sometimes is of great value. At other times, my detailed nature gets me into a whole lot of trouble. I've learned to stay calm until I have properly assessed a situation. To my dismay sometimes, my attention to detail remains a lingering weakness that still overtakes me at times. Gifts without wisdom can hurt people and situations. That's why I carefully try to navigate my responses. Trust me, this caution does not come easily for me and was especially true during Hennie's treatment. I had to keep my inside-the-room privileges intact. My diplomacy quotient was exceedingly tested during those months when only a very high score kept me a member of the "Inside Club."

Sure enough, the IV placed that night proved to be the very spot the bacteria entered his body. After a couple days, the spot became inflamed, so I alerted the nurse. The IV was replaced, but the damage had already been done, hiding inside his body where no one could see until its destruction became obvious. How crazy is that? The bacteria took refuge in the gallbladder, where it wreaked such havoc that the organ was left destroyed and dead.

Infection is a common complication during any hospital stay, especially in patients with open wounds, extended hospitalizations, and those who require endless needle punctures. Hennie's body had massive wounds that never got infected; countless IVs were placed, and yet this little devil crept in via one of those tiny needle holes! Kudos go to the amazing staff, though, who gave him superb care that prevented countless other possible complications.

More pictures on walls should be displayed to honor these brave health-care professionals for all the good they bring in the lives of desperately sick people. I cry as I write this paragraph in pure wonderment for the call they so diligently follow to bring healing and care to others. To put it mildly, the medical staff members were our angels who worked long hours in their godly call and nursed Hennie back to life—mostly under extreme stress. They were our heroes for sure!

Shower, Beautiful Shower

Hennie was bent over when he walked because of an invasive infection! He even had pain in that area of his body, yet he never complained or said anything. After the diagnosis, he told us so many parts of his body were in pain that one more area simply slipped by unnoticed. I am sure that was what happened, whereas another explanation might well have been that he knew the more he complained about anything, the longer he would have to stay in the hospital.

As he recovered, his first mode of transportation was a wheelchair, which finally enabled him to get around, including into a shower to feel cleansing water on his body for the first time in months. Getting him and his wheelchair into the shower was quite a feat though! All of the remaining dressings had to be removed to clean the open wounds. Washing from head to toe under running water was five-star treatment for him at the time. Finally, nice soap with lots of running water! Having a shower was a huge improvement over how he had been bathed in the trauma unit, where we held his head over the top end of the bed with plastic bags under his neck, washing his hair over a trash can to catch the water. The small things in life—like being able to wash your hair under running water—do turn out to be the big things. His first shower was a big deal.

No scrubbing anymore either. Thank God, those days were over. The showers were refreshing, even though his body was still fragile with several open wounds. Getting him in and out of clothes, wound dressings, braces and body suits was quite an undertaking—almost like taking care of a baby. The braces for the drop foot caused his regular shoes and clothes to be unsuitable. Thank God for Kmart! Baggy clothes and bulky shoes—anything sloppy and comfortable replaced his regular, well-fitting clothes. To go through this routine every day took nearly two hours, but we did what we had to do.

With all the caveats and shenanigans of Hennie's journey back to health, the second mile of faith became the norm—that extra distance all of us are at times called to walk—even when we think we have reached capacity. We found, though, that God was very present in the second mile. As a matter of fact, God lives there! The second mile and beyond is where even faith is not sufficient—where more than mere faith is required.

How About You?

What do you do when faith alone is not enough? You may have faith even though you cannot see where God is in the situation. That is when it is easy to stumble and fall away from what you once believed into a place of doubt and bitterness.

Faith alone is sometimes not enough. Peter addressed believers when he told them what needed to be added to their faith. He said God has given us promises and a divine nature as people of faith in Him. We ourselves need to add the following intangibles shared in 2 Peter:

But also for this very reason, giving all diligence, add to your faith virtue, to virtue knowledge,

To knowledge self-control, to self-control perseverance, to perseverance godliness, to godliness brotherly kindness, and to brotherly kindness love.

For if these things are yours and abound, you will be neither barren nor unfruitful in the knowledge of our Lord Jesus Christ.

For he who lacks these things is shortsighted, even to blindness, and has forgotten that he was cleansed from his old sins.

Therefore, brethren, be even more diligent to make your call and election sure, for if you do these things you will never stumble.

(2 Peter 1:5-10)

At times in life our faith is tested. Our faith will have to actively manifest the miraculous in our life in order for us to experience God's promises and live the dream He has given us.

Don't get weary, but walk it out one day at a time while adding the intangibles about which Peter talked. You'll look back in awe at how God was faithful in bringing all of His promises to pass.

Hold on!

8

Is This Ever Going to End?

Fighting the Fury of the Unexpected Complications

complication

noun: com•pli•ca•tion \ ˌkäm-plə-ˈkā-shən\

- a complexity, intricacy; especially: a situation or a detail of character complicating the main thread of a plot.

- a difficult factor or issue often appearing unexpectedly but changing existing plans, methods, or attitudes.

- a secondary disease or condition developing in the course of a primary disease or condition.

WHEN I WAS A little girl, my dad would say, "One fool at a time" when things got complicated and tempers short. He meant that it was best to deal with one problem at a time. That saying grew into wisdom to live by as I matured in life. The proper way to deal with issues is one at a time in order to give them all of our focus while systematically working to accomplish the desired result.

But that is not how life usually works. Oftentimes trouble runs in packs, as if one bad experience gives permission to the next. The nature of complications is that they arrive when least welcome during a time of pre-existing weakness. Painful situations appear at times never to end—even when we are more than ready to be done with them. It may be time to look back at how far we've come, take a breath, and move on. Never drop out of the fight though. Stay alert, ready to resist every evil thing that wants to continue to rob our lives of the destinies God has for us.

Infection Found a Way

During Hennie's recovery, the most feared and deadly complication was that his wounds would become infected. Our forever miracle is that that complication never occurred. The gallbladder infection was the first complication of Hennie's accident. Bacteria entered his bloodstream during his hospitalization, lodged in his gallbladder, and totally destroyed that organ. We were unaware of this complication until the problem was finally exposed through symptoms that thankfully guided the surgeons to the solution.

The gallbladder infection is a prime example of complication because it was pain upon pain. An already long hospital stay suddenly became even longer. Just when all of the wounds on Hennie's skin started to close up nicely, he came out of surgery with more cuts and holes in his body. We had already celebrated the removal of the last intravenous needle from his body, when one had to again be placed in his veins to deliver the multiple strong antibiotics to fight the infection. That's the very nature of complications—multiple issues going on at the same time. Just when you think you can take a breath, something else pops up to complicate matters.

An Allergic Reaction to Medicine

Two nights after his gallbladder surgery, Hennie suddenly started behaving in a very strange way. His pain was under control to the point that he was able to sleep several hours at a time. When I walked up to his bed to check on him, he abruptly grabbed my arm as if he were holding on for dear life. He appeared to be trying hard to wake up from a deep sleep or fighting to keep from falling into a state of unconsciousness. He told me he felt like he was drifting uncontrollably away from reality.

Even in the midst of all this chaos, I knew it was not in character for my husband to be afraid. Nothing in this world or out of this world, for that matter, had ever scared him in any way. Jumping from airplanes or jumping with a bungee cord had never fazed him, yet now suddenly he was afraid. Not even in the shadows of his drug-induced state was this possible.

Meanwhile, the nursing staff was not at all alarmed. They suggested we wait until the next morning to see if he was feeling better. I was very disturbed at that suggestion because no one seemed able to give me either a possible explanation for what was happening. I took the liberty to call another South African friend, a brilliant clinician who was an internist in the same town to ask if he had any idea what was happening with Hennie. Upon hearing my description of what was going on with Hennie, Mark instantly knew what the problem was. (I told you he was brilliant!) He told me to tell Hennie that sleep was his friend and that he should just close his eyes and allow himself to drift away because everything was going to be fine. I just kept repeating the phrase over and over in Hennie's ear: "Sleep is your friend, my love; just sleep."

His odd response turned out to be an allergic reaction to the antihistamine that he had been administered for a rash he had developed after surgery—another complication but a small one, thank God! To this day he has the same reaction to that medicine. Only one subsequent exposure to this drug made us realize he should probably stay away from it for the rest of his life. Well, at least that was an easy bump in the road to overcome, so we moved on.

The Knee

About a week after the gallbladder surgery, Hennie was well on his way to recovery from the impact of the surgery, with only one tube remaining in the open oozing wound. We prepared for his discharge from the hospital as soon as we were sure the infection was under control since I was planning to take care of him at home. I was comfortable with changing the dressings because the nurses had thoroughly trained me. They also instructed me in how to document the discharge in the bag attached to the wound and to report any deterioration of his condition.

However, right before he was finally released from the hospital, Hennie woke up one morning with a painful and severely swollen knee that had no apparent explanation. In light of all the issues for which he was already being treated, it took the doctors a while to determine the cause of the problem. After numerous further tests, the conclusion was that the same bacteria that had lodged in his gallbladder had also found a hiding place in his knee and he had developed osteomyelitis of the distal femur and septic arthritis of the knee joint. He was receiving multiple antibiotics at the time, yet some of those resistant germs were still alive, roaming through his bloodstream. Unlike the infection of the gallbladder that was tucked away inside the body, the symptoms of his knee infection were visible right away. Therefore, the problem could be treated immediately.

Back to surgery he went one more time, this time to drain the pus from the knee and clean out the area around the knee as much as possible. More anesthesia, more medicine, more fluid retention, more elevated white blood count. *Is this ever going to stop?*

In comparison to what had been done to him so far, this surgery seemed minor at the time. Little did Hennie and I realize osteomyelitis could also be lethal. We did not know it could require amputation or be fatal if it should spread to the blood. Minor surgery—isn't it funny how surgery is only minor when it is not yours? Surgery is never minor when you are the one to don that funky, open-in-the-back robe and get on the white, cold rolling bed! After all of the skin grafts and abdominal surgery, dealing with this additional issue created one long nightmare—one that could make anyone trying to keep count, give up.

Where is all of this going? All these different complications…is his knee going to be fine? Are the bacteria still lurking inside his body, trying to find another place to hide? What does finding rheumatoid arthritis antibodies in his knee mean? Where did that come from? Could these bacteria also affect the remaining open burn wounds? I remember questioning the doctors to no avail for answers and a prognosis of his overall health status. Many questions, but so few answers. So what's new?

Seemingly, the same demon had many aliases to hide behind, yet refused to leave Hennie's presence! The minor surgery proved to be a good fix. More and stronger antibiotics were prescribed that prevented the situation from becoming worse.

Where Is Your Tooth?

Yet another surprise took place during the knee surgery. Yes, let's call this one a surprise instead of a complication because I'm sick of complications! I walked into the room after Hennie came back from the operating room, so happy to see him. Yet one look at him made me laugh hysterically. No, I promise, this was really funny! Pitiful, yes, but absolutely hilarious. When he opened his mouth to talk to me, I saw that one of his front teeth was missing!

Are you kidding me? How did that happen? He looked like a five-year-old who just lost a tooth, but he was twenty-eight! My hysteria quickly spread in the room. We all found it oddly hilarious. We also probably needed a tension release. No one had any idea how it happened! Then Hennie started smiling with us, which made the incident even funnier. Sick body, open wounds, drains, pumps and needles attached to his body…with a big smile minus one front tooth. So sad, but the more he smiled, the harder I laughed.

When the doctor came in, the atmosphere went from funny to bizarre when he asked, "Did Hennie have two front teeth prior to surgery?" I am not lying! That is exactly what he asked me.

What I wanted to say was "Well, let me think, Yes! He definitely has had two front teeth for the entire time I've known him! It was only after the anesthesiologists stuck that big tube down his throat prior to surgery that he suddenly had only one front tooth," but I behaved myself and refrained.

After all, it was only after the surgery was over that the operating room staff realized the tooth was missing. A frantic search was conducted for the tooth, but it was never found. Or maybe it was! I can visualize a cleaning person in the middle of the night washing the operating room floor coming across a lonely tooth in some obscure place, wondering who lost or forgot a front tooth. Can you see that? This is too much!

Back in Hennie's room, the search continued. The tooth could not be found on the bed, on the floor, or anywhere in the room. Next, we were off to imaging to see if the tooth perhaps entered his lungs via the intubation tube. Again, no sign of the missing tooth. The entire scenario was very disconcerting for the staff because a missing tooth after surgery could be like a loose tiger in a busy street. Have you ever heard of such craziness?

In my own mind there was only one reason for the loss of his front tooth, which Hennie didn't find funny at the time. In my state of hilarious laughter that couldn't stop, I told him it was the devil's final blow to punch him out, but he only managed to take one tooth. It was over. No more, we were going home!

Sometimes, when things strike you as funny, you should just laugh—even if it seems unfitting at the time. I certainly did. God knew I needed a laugh. I am still amused to think of this handsome man of mine with one front tooth next to a black hole where the other one was supposed to be! Funny, yes, and thank God, also fixable.

The Chicken Leg

Another humorous story I'll never forget is the time a group of people from the church brought groceries to the hospital for me to take home. That year at Thanksgiving time, our church included our family when food baskets were given out to needy families. They were so kind to bring us chicken, since we had yet to feast on turkey.

Yep, believe it or not, no turkey! We obviously still had much to learn about American culture! No one ate turkey in South Africa when we were growing up, that is, except for a few "strange people" who obviously didn't know any better. We ate lamb. Whenever there was a feast or celebration, lamb and chicken were on the menu. I suppose those who put together our basket chose chicken because it resembles turkey.

Our pastor's wife, Judy Kilpatrick, and a couple of other women from church accompanied me in the elevator to take the food to my car. As we stood in the elevator with several other people, I noticed them staring perplexedly at Judy who was holding the food. Then I saw the reason for their looks—a raw chicken leg had found its way out of the bag and was dangling at the bottom of the sack of groceries in her arms.

A raw chicken leg in a hospital elevator full of people? Oh my, was that sight funny! Or was I in such a desperate need for anything remotely comical that I doubled over laughing? I didn't know, but neither did I care! We laughed so hard that all of us were about to roll on that elevator floor laughing. The people around us must have thought we were certifiably crazy. We joked about the hospital being a scary place—even for a dead chicken. After all, the chicken's attempt to escape the bag was as if the chicken had said, "If you don't take me out of here, I'm going to get out of this bag and walk out all by myself!" Those thoughts only added to the craziness. It may not have been true for the chicken, but that was exactly how the rest of us felt at the time!

Home for Real

Ma Leen's fantastic cooking, including the best curry and rice, along with custard and melktert (South African milk pie), greeted us when we got home. We were finally home! Hennie could breathe the fresh outside air for the first time in months. We could not have been happier. His journey had been a long road home with a hospital discharge date that kept moving farther away instead of getting closer.

When we went home, the gallbladder surgery incision was still a gaping wound that had to be packed with gauze to allow the infection to ooze out instead of being trapped inside of the body. The gauze packing also prevented the wound from closing prematurely while still infected, which would have caused festering bacteria to wreak more havoc and destruction. His body had to heal from the inside out, and the only way for that to happen was to keep the wound from closing. The drainage tube, which was also still in the wound, was attached to a bag which collected the secretions. I had to clean out the bag regularly to document the drainage and to have samples cultured. Trust me, the procedure sounds gross, but I was so happy for any bit of yellow gunk that came out of his body instead of staying inside!

My husband's intense patient care needs became a normal part of our lives. Our daily routine included feeding Hennie the most calorie-rich diet possible because the skin needed ample calories to grow. He didn't have a good appetite yet, but we loaded him up with bacon, fortified drinks, and any other food he was willing to take. We would worry about a healthy diet again sometime in the future. Hennie didn't mind that part at all! The more bacon, without guilt, that is, the better, right?

Besides the food, we were in a constant cycle of dispensing and taking medications, getting him out of the pressure suit, helping him shower, dressing the wounds, packing the incision, smothering his body with lotions, and then helping him back into the pressure suit. Then we made sure everything was sterilized for the next shower escapade. Medical appointments were almost a daily occurrence, since he was not completely healed and barely in a condition to be home in the first place. He had never had so much attention from me in his life. Between him and Yolandie, our two-year-old, I had my hands full to keep everybody fed, clean, happy, medicated, and healthy. Yolandie and I were happy though because she had her daddy home, I had my husband back, and life was finally getting better.

After Ma Leen left for South Africa, friends from church and school offered the most amazing support system I could have asked for. Slowly but surely Hennie gained strength. By the spring of the next year, we were able to get out more often to enjoy his recovery. He was still in a wheelchair, but it didn't hold us back. We went out, even if it was just a trip to the mall. Yolandie would hop onto his lap for a fun ride, rolling through the mall. This was the kind of scene we had never dreamed of playing out in our lives, but it did. We made the most of it as best we could.

New Season, Bright Future

Looking back after the accident, I can truly say that we got to live the life we dreamed of living and more. God is good! To think that all this really happened is almost too overwhelming, but how God restored and redeemed what was abruptly stolen that horrible Friday in September has been amazing. Many good things followed; God has been more than faithful to us.

Medicine Stayed in the Family

The way medicine stayed in a good way was honestly beyond our wildest dreams! Yolandie will tell you that her desire to become a doctor originated during her father's hospitalization. It seems too early for her to have retained memories when she was only two years old, but she did. She recalls our walks down the hallways of Santara Norfolk General Hospital where life-size pictures of doctors, nurses, technicians, and patients decorated the walls. Their stories of helping others get well made a lasting impression on her vulnerable, pure, brilliant little mind.

During those long months that Hennie was in the hospital, Yolandie and I took frequent walks down those hallways. We admired the staff who took care of her daddy so he could get well and come home. Some of the pictures were of technicians and nurses she recognized from seeing them in Hennie's unit. I have already shared that I thought of the whole team that took care of Hennie as our angels. Yolandie noticed, and she was deeply impacted.

The Nuss family became like our family, with Dr. Don winning over Yolandie's admiration from the start. Well, maybe Tessa was the one who won her over first, but Don made a profoundly lasting impression on Yolandie's heart. He made medicine attractive by his deep devotion to the call and contagious appreciation for science, as well as his determination to make life better for those in need of healing. As one of the most brilliant doctors we've ever met and unwavering in his love for God and family, he became the person Yolandie wanted to be. Even at that young, impressionable age, God used the Nuss family to sketch the blueprint for part of Yolandie's future. They will never take any credit for who Yolandie is today, but the proof is in the pudding!

Could we ever have dreamed that our little princess had a destiny of becoming a doctor some day? Did we ever consider that seeing her daddy suffer was going to make her instead of break her, like some well-meaning friends warned us could happen? His suffering propelled her to become the godly, smart, competent, and beloved physician she is today, honored to be part of the stories of healing, comfort, and care in the lives of countless people. Many times for someone to become successful, someone else has to suffer. Our daughter's sincere love for people causes more patients to request her for their primary care than she's able to accommodate. She does not think she's all that, but as her mom I may, because she is. More than grateful and more than words can say, we give God all the glory for turning our mourning into dancing in so many ways.

Two Sons

Tears well up in my eyes when I think of our two sons who were born in the years following the accident. We were fighting for Hennie's life. While surviving by itself was a miraculous, wonderful gift, God is a God of more than enough. He had more in store for us than we could imagine at the time.

We have two very handsome sons whose very existence is a constant reminder of the mercy of God. That they are a part of our family keeps us in awe of God's fullness of time and of how He works all things together for the good when we keep our eyes on Him. We never deserved any of it, but God gave us beauty for ashes with love we never knew existed. He was not obligated to do anything. By His grace alone, we were able to keep steady in faith until we found ourselves in a place of full restoration—not perfection, because nothing in this world is perfect, but full restoration. We adore our boys, who are now men! What an honor we were given to rear them, especially after such a grave incident almost took their future before they could live it.

Niel was born almost three years after Hennie's accident. The pregnancy was a time of celebrating life again. We could hardly wait to meet another brand-new, beautiful human being God was adding to our family. The joy Niel brought to our lives was over the top as we welcomed him into our home. He was an adorable little baby who stole our hearts from his first breath. We soon found we also had a brave little fighter on our hands by the way he overcame the medical challenges he had to face from a very young age. In each instance, he has surpassed the expectations of the medical community while teaching us a level of love that goes deeper than words could ever say. He gave us much delight through all the stages of growing up as a loving, caring little boy, always aware of the needs of others. We called him our miracle baby, as we witnessed time and time again how he rose to each challenge, overcoming one obstacle after another.

Today he desires to live a life pleasing to God, with sincere love for the Lord. He is a wonderful son to us and grew strong in his own unwavering faith in God to complete every good work He has started in his life. Our hearts are forever bigger and better because of Niel. To this day he continues to display the enduring goodness of God, coupled with the heart of a champion. He is the hero in our family for sure!

Heinz, our third child, is our gift from God who brought yet another picture of God's goodness into our lives. Life in the Becker family would never have been the same without him. He would much rather have been the first-born, the leader, the eldest, but to us he is perfect with his can-do tenacious spirit. He is a touch from heaven who made our family complete, especially after doctors told us not to have any more children because of the unknown cause of Niel's medical challenges. But God had Heinz in His heart from the start—long before he came to ours. Welcoming this beautiful little baby into our world brought joy upon joy. No words can describe what a gift he is to us, as well as the honor it was to rear this adventurous, fun-loving child.

His greatest accomplishment in life, though, is his decision to live life God's way. His devotion stood the test of worldly pressure early in his young life, which makes us incredibly proud of him. For some reason, God allowed him to face several painful disappointments early in life that could have left him heartbroken and bitter but instead made him stronger and wiser. We want him to be around all the time because no family celebration is the same without him. He currently lives in another city, so we have resolved to give him time and space to live out his dreams and adventures…for now.

Our sons could have been taken away from us before they were even conceived, but God had a plan. We simply don't know the extent of God's amazing plans for us. In times of disappointment, don't make hasty decisions, don't believe your future is ruined. Instead, power through the tough spots until you see how God unveils something beautiful. He turns ashes into beauty, mourning into dancing. Not always in the way we anticipated, but in time, He does make everything beautiful—even more beautiful than you could have imagined. To us, pain truly gave room to gain.

The Gallbladder Finale

Allow me to conclude the saga of the infected gallbladder. At the time of the surgery, the organ was unrecognizably marred by the infection and, therefore, could not be removed successfully. No further procedures were done for Hennie had no lingering symptoms once the organ had healed. Doctors do not like to cut people who are symptom-free! Eleven years later, his body finally decided it was time to rid itself of the useless, calcified lump of what was once his gallbladder. After presenting some uncomfortable symptoms, it was removed surgically. Thank God for the ending of that story.

Life will continue to bring challenges, even complications; nonetheless, the lessons learned and the victories won should never be forgotten. Pain makes you bitter or better, or so they say. Even if the situation is bitter right now, it will still get better. It's never too late. Where you are or have been is not keeping you from where you are going. On the contrary, it is preparing you for what is ahead.

People used to tell me that our trials were preparing us for ministry. Sometimes, in my pain, I wished they would have shut up. (I do mean that in a very nice way.) I sometimes found it difficult to see goodness in the future while trapped in our present pain. I never walked away from God, though I definitely experienced the frailty of my human strength when the evil of darkness relentlessly lingered. On occasion, I even told God that in case all this was happening in order for me to help others, I was resigning that job because it was too painful. Trust me, I wanted to quit. How I thank God that He never took those Monday morning resignations seriously. Instead, He covered me with mercy that stretched further than the end of my rope.

> *For as the heavens are high above the earth, so great is His mercy toward those who fear Him; As far as the east is from the west, so far has He removed our transgressions from us As a father pities his children, so the LORD pities those who fear Him. For He knows our frame, He remembers that we are dust.*
>
> (Psalm 103:11-14)

How About You?

Have you ever experienced a bad situation that became worse when you thought it wasn't possible? Did something additional happen to complicate an already complicated battle? That's what complications are—a double whammy that makes an already dire situation worse, zapping the last bit of energy out of you. They are different from consequences, which are the results of actions or the effects of a cause. Complications make an already bad situation worse.

You have three options when dealing with complications:

1. Make sure they don't happen.

Precautions can be taken to prevent situations from getting worse or stirring up more of the same. Complications can be prevented in many cases. Medicine is one example where instruments and work areas are sanitized to prevent obvious complications. When you are sick, you take care of yourself to prevent further sickness or something worse that might have a way into your body when your immune system is already compromised and taxed.

It is much the same way with many things in life, so use wisdom to prevent a situation from getting worse. Take your cues from what you are dealing with to close the doors to further damage. Perhaps you are dating the wrong person or are in a relationship that is already problematic. If you don't take precautions, it will get worse. It could be that you have slight health issues that are already bad for you, but if you don't do anything about them, they will only grow worse. You can prevent many diseases by taking the right action. It could involve a situation with your kids. They may have chosen the wrong friends or embraced bad habits, but the situation is still tolerable for the moment. Complications breed in already existing problems, so the sooner you take action to circumvent further damage the better.

Taking preventive action requires tough love in many cases, as well as a healthy outlook on the logical outcome of a situation. If you wait until bad grows worse, your problems will be much bigger. This is so true with rearing kids. When they are two years old and talk back to you, the incident may seem humorous. The video you post may even go viral. When that same child comes to you at age sixteen with a pregnant girlfriend to whom he never intends to commit, you will experience complications that might have been prevented.

We should not turn into paranoid people but at the same time, we should use wisdom in all areas of our lives—with money, friendships, marriage, rearing kids, and our health. Take preventive action. Ask God to help you find wisdom so you will know how to take action before bad gets worse. "Prevention is better than cure," said Desiderius Erasmus, a Christian scholar. When you see a bad situation, make sure to institute boundaries or do whatever you can to prevent complications. When God is the center of your life, He will direct you during painful circumstances—even when it's time to back off and do nothing!

While Hennie was severely ill, we had to wear masks and gowns around him to prevent his being exposed to more germs that could have taken him from being deathly ill to actually dying. Wounds had to be dressed with extreme care and cleanliness in order to prevent complications.

Complications are exactly that—developments, entanglements, snags, problems; they create more layers of evil to the point where you may be able to do nothing about them but let them run their course.

2. Make them go away.

You may have a bad situation on your hands that has already produced complications. Many fires may be burning at the same time, leaving you confused or frustrated with what is happening. You can't believe that things got even worse when you already thought they were bad. You may be shocked that the person you thought was your friend and hurt you before, has now hurt you again. That insult upon injury caught you totally by surprise because you never thought it would happen—not again.

You may have had health issues for a while but never heeded wise counsel. You kept eating junk, and now you have to take strong medication that again will bring another set of complications to your body. Possibly you saw your child acting like a brat, but you chose to fix the issue with more toys so the little darling would like you. Now the child has done the very thing you feared—accumulated mountains of debt, lied to you, or manipulated you into a compromising situation. What do you do now?

There are two sides to this coin. On the one hand, you need to be ready to take immediate action and do whatever it takes to fix the problem. On the other hand, you need to be wise to know when it's time to back off and do nothing. The choice is tough love on the one side versus giving the person or situation love and space in order to recover.

Tough love would mean addressing the situation no matter how much it may hurt. Many times boldness with knowing your rights will be the way to fight complications, in the physical realm as well as spiritually. You may have to confront your boss or family member or get with God while going to war in the heavenlies. But be willing to do the hard thing, and, oh, my, you might even have to fast! What a thought! Jesus said that there are times when fasting and prayer is your only option to victory. Be aware not to become weird or flaky either, fighting devils behind every bush and becoming a person no one wants to be around. God may want you to fight with more love instead of tough love, so get with God to hear from Him.

When we are hurt on multiple fronts at the same time, it is especially easy for us to act irrational in some of our responses. Therefore, not doing this alone is crucial; stay accountable to a sound, healthy person or to people who truly love you and who can be honest with you. Enduring seasons of war may get weird, but remember only God can save anyone—not you. You may have to intercede, you may have to change the rules, and you may have to begin or end relationships. However, stay in faith, knowing that you need God. He will fight your battles for you, but not while you are on the couch eating donuts. He wants you to get busy with what He is doing, and then He will come alongside you and make the difference.

3. Make the best of it.

At times you will be forced to deal with the complications of a bad situation for the rest of your life. The way you choose to respond will affect the quality of the rest of your life. Making the best of the situation may be tough initially, but just take a breath; you are not alone. With God at your side, make the best of it and find a new way of doing things.

Hennie has a lot of scar tissue on his legs that no longer has hair follicles or sweat glands. They were burned away in some areas or totally absent in some skin-grafted locations. After his recovery, he discovered that when the blood circulation in his legs increased during exercise, the itching and burning were unbearable. Realizing something had to change, he discovered new ways to exercise. If the problem is permanent, make the best of it!

I know you also have scars in your life. These areas of past complications healed for the most part but never went away. Some people have to deal with huge complications on a daily basis for the rest of their life. What do they do? What do you do? Make the best of it— whatever that may mean to you. No, it isn't fair. Trust me, I know! Coming to grips with those things that remain may be extremely hard, but much grace is available from God! He will give you the courage to make the best of it.

In situations involving permanent complications, you will have two huge enemies:

Guilt

Guilt will eat you alive, leaving you cynical as well as negative. Guilt breeds more guilt and, as a result, you'll be oversensitive in taking the blame for things that were never your fault. Guilt is a dark slippery slope that binds you up in all kinds of fears. Make peace with the complications you may have caused or think you caused. Deal with them before God; forgive others, forgive yourself, but move on. Doing so may take time, but please know that God has not intended for you to live in guilt. He has taken your guilt on Himself, it is nailed to the cross. He redeemed your mistakes in order for you to no longer feel guilty! He has done your time. You are free!

Loneliness

Complications that do not go away will change your life. They will set you apart as someone with a unique experience to which not everyone may relate. You may feel that no one understands, which can be painful. Despite that feeling, don't push away others because you are in pain or your life has changed. Don't alienate yourself—even if you do feel like an alien.

Loneliness is a vicious monster; therefore, you'll have to get out of your place of comfort to connect with other people. Somewhere, someone needs you no matter what you are going through. Pray. Ask God who should be your friends and with whom you should spend time. Even if there is only one person who understands you, be grateful for that one. You don't need a crowd to find happiness or satisfaction in life. Love those you are called to love, but also reach out to someone you don't yet know. Allow others to love you and to be your friends—even if you think they have no idea of what your life is really like.

Stand Up—One More Time

My prayer for you is that you will find comfort and strength in dealing with layers of pain and that God will pick you up from any place of despair in which you may find yourself. Stand up one more time; you'll see that every dark cloud has a silver lining. Every night brings the dawning of a new day. Take what you have today and make the best of it!

9

No Calm After the Storm (Part 1)

Surviving the Trauma Even After the Fight Is Won

THE FIRST TIME *IT* happened was in my sleep. I woke up early one morning in the middle of a dream in which Hennie was engulfed in flames. He was in a death struggle to get out of it, but no matter how hard I tried, I could not help him. The flames rolled right in front of my face, leaving me deeply disturbed upon waking. My heart pounded as if a horse were running in my chest. I could hardly breathe.

Relief flushed over me when, after a couple moments, I realized I was only dreaming. I turned over in bed and scooted up against Hennie's back, holding him as tightly as I could. Tears trickled down my cheeks as I lay frozen, gripping his healed body. At that moment, I felt suspended between two realities—the warm body I held in my arms versus the one I had seen engulfed in an insatiable inferno only a minute ago. The better-case scenario was real, thank God!

Dread Found a Way In

As Hennie's recovery continued, I did not realize how dread had crept into my heart through the wounds that were far from healed— the wounds no one could see, the unseen wounds I didn't know I had. Somehow the traumatic experience had attained a sick grip on my life, turning each new day into a game of defense against what could possibly go wrong next or cause pain. Bad things had happened before, I reckoned, so another could happen again at any moment. Every new day I found myself living in dread that someone I loved could get hurt—again or worse.

What a way to live! It is no way to live! No one ever chooses to live

157

like I was living! Rather, a person gets caught in a trap set in place by painful past experiences. Is there a way out? The sad truth is that when you are in the middle of a battle with dread, all your energy is spent on what taunts you. Dealing with worst-case scenarios every day grows exhausting. Finding a way out seems an option outside the scope of your ability, this anxiety enters your life through logical thinking and natural progression.

Trust me, it's not as if you welcomed this dread into your life after it came knocking at your door one sunny afternoon. No! This evil stronghold results from a real experience after which you try to protect yourself from more pain—or to soothe the pain and feel better. It's natural.

Of course, you should fear flames burning on your body. Naturally, you should do whatever you can never to let it happen again, right? Yes, but this fear is not supposed to consume your life. My natural response to the pain heightened uncontrollably long after the danger was gone. Before I knew it, I was overwhelmed with a monster that seemed stronger than I was. I neither recognized my fear as a threat nor knew I could or should be free from it—not initially.

No one knew about the growing fears with flashbacks that tormented me. I suppressed my fears with the abundance of responsibilities in my life at the time. Hennie was returning to normal activities, while I was sinking under a heavy cloud that settled over my soul.

Looking back, I realize I had been in defensive mode for so long, powering through my days with such tenacity, that pushing through another day was normal for me. Here I was with symptoms, such as nightmares, negativity, fear, dread, sadness, etc., revealing I had indeed been living anything but a normal life. I felt as if my inner world had turned against me; my thought life became a constant source of dread.

Clueless, Yet Stuck

I didn't like what I was experiencing. At first, I was even clueless about post-traumatic stress or any kind of stress for that matter. Before this interruption in our lives, I saw stressors as mere hurdles that needed to be conquered or as challenges you figured out how to meet, work through and move past. As a matter of fact, I had little empathy with people who always seemed to be uptight about things. I had never been a moody person nor had I experienced major traumas, so I expected others to snap out of whatever was bothering them—until I could not snap out of it—at least not out of this one.

Multitudes of people on the planet never get help, recover, or settle into a place of peace after trauma. In fact, suffering under the impact of traumatic disappointment for a lifetime is quite possible. I've ministered to too many people who have been unable to find their way out of the forest of doom where a broken life left them behind.

This lack of recovery, which is deeply troubling and distressing to me, is also the reason I am willing to walk through my past pain with you one more time. I wish I could sit right next to you at this moment and listen to your heart. I would say to you, "There is a path to healing no matter what you've been through! Scars you'll have, most of us do have them, but the wounds will close up, offering you a new lease on life."

There is help if you feel hopeless; that help cannot be found within your own human resource or power but is found in the power of Jesus Christ. That is where it was for me!

Where Was My Help?
It was not in a friend,
    although we all need friends.
It was not in creating drama,
    although some may be unavoidable.

It was not in angry gossip, although when in pain we all stumble
    over that rock.
It was not in chemicals,
    although medicine is a needed tool at times.
It was not in sweeping it under the carpet,
    although some things need to be simply ignored.
It was not in a pity party,
    although those really help if kept under five minutes.
It was not in comparison to the lives of others,
    although it's good to learn from others' victories.
It was not in self-help,
    although tough decisions had to be made.
It was not from blaming myself or someone else,
    although I had to take responsibility for my responses.
It was not in behavior modification,
    although that is ultimately needed.
It was not from a source or person on earth,
    although we need human resources at times.
It was **all** God.

Looking back over the last thirty years, I can see that if not for the grace of God, I could have become a bitter, nothing-can-please-me woman, constantly putting pressure on others to make me happy; high maintenance, yet low energy; pretend-it's-all-okay person, yet deeply discontented—unable to love or be loved. If you've been through life-altering pain, this type of person is not difficult to be—even nicely hidden on the inside where no one can see. Embracing this persona destines us for a life of darkness on earth; nothing gets clean or better all by itself, but requires effort and intervention to progress. I needed spiritual soul intervention, which is exactly what I found in the presence of God.

I Ran to God

I have always been convinced that everything we need that pertains to life and godliness is in the Word of God. I found answers in matters I could understand, comfort when I couldn't, and wisdom to know the difference. This golden thread that became my global positioning system when nights were dark has remained true in my life. I have by no means arrived, but I have navigated fierce storms, and now I get to enjoy the fruit of many seeds planted in darkness. There is more seed in the ground, answers not yet seen, but the outcome is up to God. In the meanwhile, each day is a gift with more than enough beauty to enjoy, and more than enough grace from God to get through the tough spots as well!

God never leaves us or forsakes us; when we run to Him, He never disappoints. God's power is greater than the pangs of a tormented soul—no matter the degree of the pain. We all experience pain, whether public or private. God knows it all. He is the safe place that has already provided for every need we may have. Some hurts or injuries take a long time to overcome, while others may go instantaneously when God walks on the scene. Either way, He never leaves!

Consider Our Frame

During our time on earth, it is helpful to consider our frame—how we were created, our divine design. We live in extremely complex organic tents, crowned with the gift of our own will, with flexible emotions cleverly programmed for spiritual interaction. Remember that our minds hold onto experiences, retaining detailed information—even when we don't want to. We sometimes need to overcome some of these features in our DNA that can be very hard or even impossible to override. When life happens, we easily get stuck with default settings. We effortlessly follow paths of impulse or previously trailed pathways of response that won't easily go away.

Why is it so hard to let go? Why is life seemingly upside down at times? From our earthly perspective, the good things tend to end badly, while the bad things often won't go away. Is this a bad joke or are we simply doomed to fail for some mysterious reason?

The human body is a wonderful machine, carefully fashioned with every feature serving a very specific purpose. We were created to commune with God, to connect with others, to love; therefore, we are hardwired to remember people and how they make us feel, as well as retain facts, skills, and habits. This ability, which is our greatest asset as well as our fiercest enemy, transforms our memories into spontaneous or instinctive thinking patterns. When the thought patterns are good, they are pleasurable but devastating when they are not. Meant to help us hold onto the beauty of life's experiences, thoughts sometimes double up as the cause of the greatest pain we can possibly experience—the pain of broken hearts, crushed dreams, lingering disappointment or fear of sudden disaster.

The Bible says we are created in God's image with eternity in our hearts. God is a Spirit who lives forever; so are we. For a brief moment in time here on earth, we are subject to the ramifications and limitations of our earthly suits, our flesh, yet deep inside we are wired for timeless existence. We therefore have capacities to dream, hope, believe and trust. Wonderfully and fearfully made, we humans are! But somewhere, something went very wrong. These traits became subject to evil manipulation that turned our pure nature against our own destiny.

Satan has been given authority here on earth to seize the vulnerability of our remarkable human qualities. So in perfect tactical warfare fashion, he turned our own abilities against us. The great pretender, twister of truth, sly swindler extraordinaire, will arrest any part of our being that is not redeemed by the blood of Jesus Christ.

Malfunction

Yes, a malfunction occurred when mankind chose to eat the forbidden fruit in the garden of Eden. A system breakdown followed that caused these beautiful machines to turn against themselves. We are now hardwired to hold on to negative, painful memories, where we were originally created to house God encounters, as was the case before the fall of man in Genesis 3. The malfunction separated us from God's original plan.

Anything from an offensive word or action by another person to the shock and devastation of any of life's traumas, now becomes lodged in our thinking pathways. The more we use these negative thinking patterns, the stronger they become. Our minds follow the path of least resistance, ingraining habits that form from a young age. Habits are necessary for growth, crucial in functioning here on earth; they are our most amazing asset and yet our worst enemy as they are very hard to break.

The Fight Was Not Over After the Trauma Was

Little did I know the fight was not over. Past battles had made me stronger but not immune to more. More effort was needed on my part—even after the dust settled, since memories had burned paths for future torment into my soul. I didn't know what flashbacks were until I started waking up in the middle of the night, seeing Hennie ignited in flames as clear as day right in front of my face. Some flashbacks turned into tormenting nightmares, laced with fiery demonic images.

I was super-strong in the heat of the battle, but I fell apart afterward. I was a woman of faith in tight relationship with God, so how could this happen? How is this possible? I trusted God, witnessed miracles, and kept the faith, yet my broken heart was overwhelmed with questions I didn't know how to ask.

This aftermath or delayed weakness included physical exhaustion and emotional wounds as well as a spiritual weakening, which left me quite chaotic. I had no idea what was going on, for I had never before experienced depression or any other form of mental weakness—not even PMS. I was not very emotional or dramatic either, but able to ride out tough situations—until life happened. I was forced to deal with heart issues that had the power to change it all and steal the resilience I once had, leaving me emotionally crippled and weak.

Life has a way of introducing us to our own human frailties. We all experience different degrees of pain, which should not be judged or compared to that of another. Pain is pain. Pain may look very different for different people, yet no one can rightfully judge the degree to which it hurts.

Good Fear, Bad Fear

Fear is not bad; in fact, this crucial inherent emotion is intended to keep us from harm by guiding us to safe decisions. We are also to fear God; having a holy reverence for God is the beginning of all wisdom. Yet fear is a powerful trap when warped by our carnal minds. Unhealthy fear is a twisted version of the kind we were created to hold; the Bible calls it a trap. Pain and suffering often flip a switch in our souls, making it seem like an angry giant has awakened in our minds to keep us constantly suppressed through impending terror or failure.

Unhealthy Fear:
Strives to play a larger than needed role in our life
Shows up via symptoms not initially evident to the victim
Promises to keep us safe but turns to torment
Overrides logic until it becomes the litmus test for life events
Causes the victim to back off too easily
Says, "Do not take any chances; you'll fail."

Avoids anything that could possibly hurt
Rules and distorts the victim's thoughts, responses and actions
Promises to protect its obedient victim from more pain
Keeps wounds festering rather than forming healed scars
Promotes logic resulting in overthinking and overanalyzing
Keeps freedom at bay as it promotes constant defense
Enables wounds to continue festering for a lifetime
Produces hypersensitivity to potential pain
Causes overreaction under threat
Easily takes up offenses, assuming worst-case scenarios
Blames others for any discomfort
Demonizes people as the cause of pain
Breeds more negativity
Leaves the victim feeling disenfranchised
Promotes suffering from short tempers and anger outbursts
Thrives in self-destructive behavior
Renders its victims fainthearted, powerless, alienated and controlling.

These symptoms are often the result of physical and emotional pain, and need healing.

Satan pounces on pain and weakness like a heartless bully. God's will is not for anyone to suffer under these notions, nor does it evidence victorious living. The God factor—God's supernatural miraculous intervention—is the answer to this frailty we all carry in our earthly suits.

For God has not given us a spirit of fear but of power and of love and of a sound mind. (2 Timothy 1:7)

Paul contrasts the spirit of fear with someone filled with God's Spirit. When we demonstrate power to do what we are called to do, know we are loved, and are able to think clearly, we operate in freedom as opposed to fear.

What do we do? How do we win this battle? God's Word answers these questions.

> *Therefore submit to God. Resist the devil and he will flee from you.* (James 4:7)

Note that we have to submit to God first of all and then resist the devil, and he has to flee. Our minds need to be renewed by the Word of God as well, so we know to what we are submitting! Note the importance of submission to God in living victoriously. We will always have areas in our lives where God is still at work, yet living in surrender to God brings peace—no matter the circumstances. Take a moment to read all of James chapter 4. This is a battle we have to fight. We need to resist oppression, but it presupposes total submission to God.

Love Is the Cure

During this time, a spiritual revelation God brought to life for me was that perfect love casts out fear. That verse made all the difference to me. I knew this truth as Scripture and believed it as fact, but I needed a fresh understanding and infusion of God's love to manifest its truth in my life. Consider how this truth applies to a committed love relationship between a man and a woman. Perfect love cannot exist while fear is present. For instance, if either one has a constant fear of being hurt or cheated, the couple will never enter into the heart of a true love relationship.

Fear quenches love, resulting in unwanted emotions in relationships that cause you to judge others negatively, to act reserved, to be defensive, to build walls instead of bridges, to be distrustful, and to expect the worst, while leaving you impotent and fruitless. Love trusts, is open and vulnerable, chooses to believe the best, hopes for better days and takes a chance for deep connection. The same is true in our relationship with God. Ponder the love of God, get to know God better, ask Him for a fresh revelation of His love for you. You will find Him worthy of your trust. Seek Him. He will not disappoint.

> *There is no fear in love; but perfect love casts out fear, because fear involves torment. But he who fears has not been made perfect in love.* (1 John 4:18)

I could find no solace in the reasons for the trauma nor peace in understanding why it all happened. I had a choice either to set my life on a quest to get all the answers attached to the pain, or to turn to God. Alas, knowledge was not my answer. In walking with God we do gain knowledge that grows our faith, but knowledge alone has never saved anyone. Knowledge without God's perspective leads to a path away from God—away from the miraculous supernatural interventions that truly heal our souls. Recognizing this truth brings me to the next step in overcoming fear, which is found in the case of Adam and Eve.

Choose Your Tree

In Genesis 3:6, Eve was tempted to eat the fruit from the only tree that God had forbidden to them—the tree of the knowledge of good and evil. She listened to the snake, saw that the fruit of the tree was good for food, was pleasant to the eyes and was desirable to make one wise, so she ate.

Not much has changed, has it? We still think that by intellectually judging good and evil, we can attain the highest form of life on earth. As a result, we chase after satisfying our minds with understanding in order to attain greatness, while the Bible clearly teaches that the only true wisdom is from God. For instance, we can easily follow a quest to understand all of the issues of life, while in the process we forget to really live. We stand to miss out on the joys of life, alienate the ones we should love, all the while growing further away from God.

God wants us to be wise. He gave us understanding and crowned us with brilliant intellect, yet the real truth is that the fear of God is the beginning of all wisdom. In trying to satisfy our need for understanding everything apart from God, we will gain a measure of success, yet never arrive at the knowledge fully able to satisfy our fleshly understanding or save us from harm.

Adam and Eve ate and died. From that moment forward, they started aging on the way to the death of their organic bodies that had initially been created to live forever. The worst part was that from the moment they sinned, they were separated from the presence of God they had enjoyed up to then. They were expelled from the garden that God had created for them and denied access to the tree of life. If God had not exercised that judgment, but allowed them to stay alive forever in that same form, imagine how wicked we would all be today! Earthly death was necessary to end the trail of sin, so we could re-enter God's presence in eternity with new bodies, purchased by the blood of His Son, Jesus Christ.

This is a deep analogy, but in God's world, everything means something. The physical matter we observe are shadows of what is real with God, object lessons in eternal matters. God, who is a Spirit, expresses and shows Himself through what He created in the physical world we see.

For since the creation of the world His invisible attributes are clearly seen, being understood by the things that are made, even His eternal power and Godhead. (Romans 1:20)

Just like Adam and Eve, we also dine from the tree of the knowledge of good and evil when we act on our physical desires. So we also eat and die—death to the destiny God has for us—our destiny here on earth as well as after we die. During our earth time, when we eat from this the tree, we fail to live a full life in faith. Living in faith is to live in what we cannot see, believing every word of God. Living outside of faith in God and His Word will result in a life outside of all the benefits and goodness of God. What are His benefits? Here is a taste:

And forget not all His benefits: Who forgives all your iniquities, Who heals all your diseases, Who redeems your life from destruction, Who crowns you with lovingkindness and tender mercies, Who satisfies your mouth with good things, So that your youth is renewed like the eagle's. (Psalm 103:2-5)

But without faith it is impossible to please Him, for he who comes to God must believe that He is, and that He is a rewarder of those who diligently seek Him. (Hebrews 11:6)

Why live in faith? Why is it impossible to please God without faith? Why does it please God when we live by faith? The answer to this questions is that there is much more to life than we understand. God is saying that we have access to things we can't see while we live here on earth. Living without believing there is a realm beyond our physical senses limits our knowledge to the physical realm, gained through our physical senses. When we live only by what we see, we live a life much smaller than God intended. God's will is for us to have access to His presence here on earth and to enter into eternity with Him when we leave this world.

When Adam and Eve sinned in the garden, God shed the blood of an animal to cover their nakedness. This act was a shadow of the Lamb—Jesus Christ, the Son of God, who came and died to restore us to God—being slain to cover the sin of mankind. The way back to God's presence came through the death of Christ. To be His followers, we have to die daily to our own desires, accept Jesus Christ as the One who redeemed us, and so enter into eternal life. Our earthly death is the final transition, the door, the last enemy that stands between us and eternal life with Him.

> After sin entered this world,
> there was no more life without death,
> no win without pain,
> no victory without a fight,
> no joy without sorrow,
> no pleasure without sacrifice,
> no prize without a race,
> no mountaintop without a climb,
> no party without preparation,
> no growth without planting a seed.
> Christ came to give us
> life from death,
> success at the end of pain,
> victory in our battles,
> joy after our sorrow,
> a prize at the end of a race,
> mountaintop experiences after a climb,
> celebration after much toil,
> fruit from the seeds we sow.

God allowed Adam and Eve to eat from the many trees in the garden, including another specifically mentioned, the Tree of Life. Obedience would have kept them in close communion with God and allowed them to live forever. Think about what that meant—no death, no aging, and direct access to God. Why then did God give them a choice if He knew what was best for them? Without choice, we could never experience real love, since love is a choice. Without choice, we'd be mere robots, far from the image of God.

How do we eat from the tree of life today? We choose to follow a path that leads to life by what we say, by acting in a way that offers grace and by living a life that brings forth fruit for others to enjoy. We choose to speak life even when there is pain, speak hope where despair abounds, believe for better days when nights are very dark, think the best of others, expect goodness to come into our lives by avoiding the wide path of judgment, and refusing to focus on worst-case scenarios. We choose the narrow, sometimes lonely path of doing the right things that will bring life into a situation.

You ultimately eat from the tree of life when you choose Jesus Christ!

He is the One who loves mankind.

He is the only One who has died because of His love for you!

He chose to die.

That is love.

10

No Calm After the Storm (Part II)

Overcoming Pain that Lingers in the Aftermath

Intervention

Flashbacks of Hennie's being enveloped in flames often occurred in my sleep, and sudden bouts of sadness would hit me at random times during the day. I had no idea what to do or how to deal with these tormenting dreams or times of great melancholy. All I knew to do was pray and bring the matter to God. Of course I chose the right solution, yet I had areas in my life that needed to line up with the will of God to complete my healing. I needed much deeper intervention than I realized.

Sometimes only a miracle can save a soul, heal wounds, restore relationships, and bring us back to a place where joy and goodness thrive. Thank God He never changes. He is the God of miracles; otherwise, why even pray or believe? Answers to life's toughest questions are not earthly but originate in the supernatural realm where God lives. Intervention came to me in the form of miracles from heaven, godly friends, and time.

I. Miracles from Heaven

Miracles from heaven happen when we arrive at the end of natural science, earthly understanding and physical resilience; then the supernatural power of God brings insight, peace and healing. God oftentimes heals us immediately, but other times our restoration requires a journey of recovery.

Trauma, disappointment and deep hurt offer a way for evil thoughts and demonic oppression to enter our minds and hearts. Let me be clear: not demonic possession if you are redeemed, but *oppression* or influence. This is the temptation addressed in an earlier chapter, when Satan, the tempter, barrages us with all kinds of evil options and actions at our disposal in times of painful weakness. These attacks do not present themselves in the form of caricature-like demons with pitchforks, but in very natural logical thoughts. Someone once said that our minds are landing strips for demonic thoughts. The battle for our soul is in our mind; therefore, the Bible teaches that our mind needs to be renewed by the Word of God. These thoughts will come, and even land, but we have to resist them by the power of Christ in us.

> *For though we walk in the flesh, we do not war according to the flesh. For the weapons of our warfare are not carnal but mighty in God for pulling down strongholds, casting down arguments and every high thing that exalts itself against the knowledge of God, bringing every thought into captivity to the obedience of Christ.* (2 Corinthians 10:3-5)

The only way we can access the supernatural power of God is through Jesus Christ. This world offers many other avenues to healing and success but, beware, all that is spiritual is not necessarily of God. Spiritual solutions are presented to us via the media, celebrities, talk-show hosts, positive thinking, behavior modification, self-help literature, medicine, and even human love. None of these are real solutions, but rather, cover-ups void of eternal truth. Nothing in this world can take the place of a personal, real, loving relationship with God through Jesus Christ. In the presence of God, nothing is impossible. One moment with God can instantly heal brokenness, align our hearts with God's will, regenerate our deep calling to purpose, and grant us fullness of life on earth. One moment in the presence of God can change a life forever.

Jesus Christ is the only way to God's redemptive power, yet different people connect with God in different ways. Jesus is always the same, but we all have different temperaments or experiences that position us uniquely to sense God's presence. Before you think this is weird, let me explain.

For some believers, music is a powerful tool to connect with God. They find solace and connection with God while making or listening to spiritual music, when they are alone or in corporate worship settings. A wonderful godly friend, who has been a missionary all of his life, loves to enjoy God's presence while listening to classical music. Let's not judge so quickly! For others, spending time in nature with the majesty of God in His creation may bring a beautiful sense of connection with God.

Another committed Christian friend grew up in a traditional church where he finds rich communion with God through liturgy and sacraments. Worship stirs his heart and brings him closer to the One he adores. Others find their best place of connecting with God early in the morning in personal devotion on the floor, in a closet, or in deep conversation with someone else about the mysteries of the Word of God. Visiting a certain place or simply reading Scripture in the afternoon breeze under a tree could stir a powerful connection with God. These pathways or places have no power in and of themselves, but they set us in a place that may help prepare our souls to hear the voice of God.

These avenues are all acceptable if they stimulate you to focus on Christ while building your heart with faith in God. Face time with Jesus is possible, and it will bring peace not confusion, revelation not isolation, openness not alienation, joy not aggravation. Goodness and mercy will follow! I am not proposing that you do a weird dance in the woods while chanting something crazy! That is obviously strange and out of context. I do encourage you to find your best way of spending time with God. In all things, always stay in alignment with the truth of God's Word.

You may find from time to time you will need a deeper connection with God—something different from your daily devotional or connect time with God. A couple of times a year or when you really feel you need it, you may want to get away alone. This time may be spent with the person who mentors you or somewhere outdoors in the forest or at the ocean where you can clear your mind in the undisturbed presence of God. If you've never taken time to connect with God, it may be time for you to plan a getaway with the distinct purpose of spending time with God. A couple of hours, a day, or a weekend will be more than worth your while.

On a daily basis though, ritual is helpful. Find a time and place in or around your home that is your special spot. This special place may be a room, a closet, or even a chair where you keep your Bible with your notebook ready. Choose a time that works for you when you can think clearly. God sees your heart. If you fall asleep each time you pray longer than two minutes, you should probably pick a better time!

Studying or reading Scripture with an open heart will set you up for miracles. The Word of God is alive, as if God speaks it every moment. The Bible contains the very breath of God. Though the Bible contains the history of the Hebrew people, it is not a history book per se, but contemporary life every moment. Pray and ask God to make the Bible clear to you as you read. Do whatever it takes to find time to spend in the Word of God.

When my children were young, my time was occupied with being a mom from dawn to dusk. I often found it difficult to find time to spend with God while I was not exhausted. I found that having my Bible in the kitchen helped a lot. I left it open on the counter just like a recipe book, so I could read even just a verse or memorize Scripture while doing chores. It works! If you can cook while reading a recipe, you can cook and read the Bible. After all, the Bible is the true bread of life! It builds your faith and reveals God's will for you, which prepares you for miracles to happen in your life.

Miracles happen in the spiritual realm before they are ever manifested in the physical world in your life. Most physical actions are the same. Before the act ever manifests, you think it in your mind where it is not visible to the naked eye. The thought is essential in order for the act to happen. You see the apple in your mind's eye well before you walk over to the basket to take it. It is much the same way with receiving from God. You read Scripture, you listen to messages, and you engage in worship, causing your heart to start believing God for the manifestations you need in your life.

This is certainly not to be identified with positive thinking. It is finding and believing the will of God, and standing in faith for it until you see it come to pass. There is no substitute for getting to know God personally through His Word. The Bible is your promise book, your living testament of what Jesus left behind for you at the time of His death. Don't miss out! It is for you. You are a beneficiary. Your name is written in the palm of His hand.

II. Godly Friends

Friendships can present influence that lead you closer to God's plan for your life or serve as a complete trap, a pitfall into dark despair.

The words of the wicked kill; the speech of the upright saves.
(Proverbs 12:26 MSG)

Do not be misled: "Bad company corrupts good behavior."
(1 Corinthians 15:33 NIV)

For you to decide how close someone gets to your heart is permissible. Distancing yourself from someone does not mean rejection or being rude in any way. Friendliness costs nothing, but friendship can be very, very expensive. I am not being judgmental when I say that some people are simply not meant to occupy a place close to your heart.

When in pain or trauma, your friendships may change, which should not come as a surprise. Some completely new godly friendships may form, while others you've had may die. Trauma has a way of sifting friends, which is okay. It happened to Jesus!

In Matthew 26:38 Jesus says, *"My soul is exceedingly sorrowful, even to death. Stay here and watch with Me."* Jesus then went off by Himself and fell on His face before God, crying out for help in His deepest time of torment. Maybe an hour later when He returned to the place where He had left the disciples, He found them sleeping. He said to Peter, *"What? Could you not watch with Me one hour? Watch and pray, lest you enter into temptation. The spirit indeed is willing, but the flesh is weak"* (Matthew 26:40-41). This was Jesus, the Son of God, with His closest friends. Sadly, they were not strong enough to stand with Him; they did not comprehend the full scope of what Jesus was going through.

Just the mere fact that Jesus disclosed He was in a death struggle when He asked for their prayer is both amazing and revealing to me. To be honest and transparent when you are hurting is good. Disclose your despair to carefully chosen close friends—the select few you can trust. Ask for help; ask for prayer but do not expect even the closest of friends to understand fully your circumstances. Don't blame them if they fail you in your darkest hour; instead, know they are willing yet human.

Wow! What a wake-up call for us with all of the conditions and expectations we place on our friends! It took Jesus' disciples until after His death to understand. Jesus had to walk out His destiny first; it is always a path of one. Walking out your destiny can be very lonely, but if you know God is with you and that you are in the middle of His will for your life, you can do it! Jesus did—even to the point of God's turning away His face from His Son for a moment! That abandonment is surely the epitome of loneliness. Jesus remained the Son of God during the dark times He was destined to walk. The same is true with us. We may have to walk out painful portions of our lives totally abandoned, but we are never alone nor forgotten by God!

That Jesus had some radical friends is quite apparent. Many other accounts in the Bible speak volumes concerning the nature of such relationships. The night when Jesus was betrayed in Gethsemane, His friends did not understand what was happening. Jesus is the Son of God; His time on earth was divine, and He functioned in the supernatural. Yet what happened at Gethsemane serves as our example in many ways. In that dark night, one of His disciples came to Him accompanied by a great multitude with swords and clubs who were there for the purpose of betraying Jesus. They came from the chief priests and elders of the people to arrest Him. Simon Peter carried a sword, and in defending Jesus, he severed the ear of one of the servants of the high priest. What a good friend he was to Jesus…maybe not.

Blood must have been flowing down his garments and an ear had to have been lying on the ground! Peter was ready to fight, and he probably assumed Jesus was as well, so they made a good team! Unlike Peter, however, Jesus stayed in character—not at all swayed by what was happening. The ear on the ground—would he heal it or not? He was after all the One who had healed everyone everywhere He went. This time was different though; He was surrounded with armed soldiers. Was He in danger of being stabbed or should He reach down to pick up the ear on the ground?

Should He even twitch while surrounded by a multitude of swords and clubs? Yes, Jesus covered the mistake of His friends in the midst of imminent danger by reaching out to the bloody ear on the ground. He picked it up and put it back where it belonged. He told Peter to put away his sword, for all who take up the sword will perish by the sword. Jesus was saying to Peter that not every battle belonged to him.

Not every threat needs a response in like kind! Peter was not re-acting the way Jesus wanted him to respond—exactly like our friends sometimes don't either. But Jesus covered His friend's mistake. He taught him that retaliation is not always in order. Peter had a sword, but it was not the time or place for a fight. Peter was to stay with Jesus. Considering how reactionary we all can get in stressful situations is eye-opening. We react in error at times, but it does not mean that we should sever the friendship. On the other hand, Jesus made Himself very vulnerable when He reached down to pick up that ear!

If I had been in that situation, things would have been different. I might have thought that the servant's ear was of much less importance than my life being in danger of death. Forget the ear; it's all about me now! But no, not Jesus—not that time. Yet His friends didn't get the example. As a matter of fact, the same friend who cut off the servant's ear ran away when Jesus was taken by force and escorted to the high priest. In actuality, they all ran away! In my world that would mean the friendship is over, but not in Jesus' world. Peter even betrayed Jesus three times that same night, yet Jesus restored the relationship.

Some God-people may enter your life during difficult times in a way that will bring comfort to your heart or stir your faith. Other friends may be lost during tough times for many reasons. Perhaps they have too much going on in their own lives, so they have no power or inclination to walk with you during your times in the val-ley. That does not make anyone bad or ungodly, but circumstances could cause some friendship paths to grow faint or even separate. At the same time, pain can also blur your judgment and allow ungodly influences in your life.

How Do You Recognize a Good Friend?

+ **By the way you feel after spending time with them.**
  In what state of mind do you find yourself after spending time

with a particular friend? Don't be too sensitive, but for the most part, time spent with a true friend should leave you encouraged, lifted up, and energized to trust God more. Being with a friend should not leave you feeling judged, drained, or confused. You are allowed to surround yourself with those who have a positive influence in your life. You should be concerned if you have a friend who constantly leaves you with negative impressions.

♦ **By the way they love you unconditionally.**

Not all people who walk into your world are meant to be your close friends. Not all who claim they love you actually love you unconditionally. Some may be friends, but their friendship is based on a list of conditions you have to meet. These relationships will be energized when you act in the way they expect you to act. When you mess up or don't live up their expectations, you'll be ignored or abandoned. This kind of relationship is extremely unhealthy, and unfortunately most of us have been on both sides of this equation to some degree.

If you have a friend like this, it may be time for a conversation, a renegotiation of the friendship, a reconnecting of hearts to make sure the friendship is worth saving. So consider those who really truly love you, those who stay aligned with you whether you perform correctly or mess up, as your real treasures. Don't take them for granted; fight for those friendships with all your might.

♦ **By the way they defend you when you are not around.**

This attribute is a big one. Finding or having such a friend is priceless. Loyalty is what happens when someone sticks with you, has your back, even if there are no personal benefits in the immediate situation. A true friend sees the best in you and is ready to represent you well in every circumstance. Standing up for someone whom you know is innocent of an accusation, while others judge or misunderstand that person takes grit. Saying nothing at times is easier, but remember that your silence casts a vote. Keep in mind that we all slip up and sometimes do stupid things. No one is perfect, but recurring slip-ups or repeated breaches of trust are red flags of danger ahead.

You may have friends from whom you need to distance yourself, or you may have a void of true godly people in your world. Whatever the case, you will have to do something about this situation. If you find it difficult or if you are insecure about separating from someone, discussing the matter with a confidante you can trust might be best. If you think you're going to mess it up, seek help from someone, perhaps an older, wiser person, or a spiritual leader who can give you sound godly counsel.

If you have a dire lack of friends who love you unconditionally, you should first be that kind of friend to someone else. Be to someone else the person you need in your own life. You may already know where to find friends who will be loyal. An old adage says not to eat fish at a steakhouse or tacos at a sandwich shop. Expect to find potential close friends in places with people who share your values and interests. Get out there and make it happen!

III. Time

Deep interventions come not only in the form of miracles from heaven and godly friends, but also with time—your worst enemy or your best friend. Time is crucial especially in the aftermath of trauma or pain. Some areas or issues in your life will be restored instantly, while others won't. You may not even notice how time heals, but it does—at least sometimes. Time does heal wounds, but time alone does not heal all wounds. As a matter of fact, time may reveal wounds, which initially is what happened to me. I simply assumed that life happens, then life moves on, but it didn't.

Scars, which are leftover reminders of past trauma, are actually an interesting phenomenon in the human body. Not all injuries heal in the same way. Time is always needed for the body to do what it does best, which is to heal itself. Sometimes healing takes place rapidly with barely any trace of past injury. Other times scars may heal superficially but leave the wounded one with areas that need additional care.

Such was the case with Hennie's third-degree burns. The healing continued over a period of many years. Year after year he had to wear the pressure garments in order for his skin to heal and grow properly. The deep burn areas had lost its DNA code and, therefore, the ability to regenerate as it once was. The scar tissue continued to grow for years following the accident. Without intervention over that long span, the scars would have grown out of control, forming huge clumps of point-less tissue, and leaving the body unable to perform certain functions.

Healing the heart is much the same. The process of recovery goes on long after the insult. Depending on the depth of the wound, it will require nurturing over a period of time until things become as near to normal as they are going to get. Be aware of the fact that healing needs time; allow it.

Keep in mind that trauma will also cause pain and wounds in areas other than those directly affected by the insult or damage. Those wounds usually take the most time to heal. God was faithful to send us help through someone who cared enough to bring up the subject long after most people had forgotten what we had experienced. Though awkward at first, the conversation brought deep comfort. It was a part of God's healing plan after the tragedy we went through.

We had a dear South African friend, now with Jesus, who was a missionary in Africa for most of his life. Johan Engelbrecht was our very first connection to the United States, so he frequently visited us during his travels there. He was a godly man, sensitive to the needs of others, and one who loved the leading of the Holy Spirit. During one of his visits with us several years after Hennie's accident, he asked some difficult questions that were quite appropriate at the time. He wanted to know how our marriage was doing in light of what we had been through, as well as some other issues that we faced.

The truth is that we were still having some struggles as far as our marriage was concerned. How did he know? He just did. He was wise to realize there was a time for everything, and that day was our time to open our hearts to receive the love and care we so desperately needed.

The dangers of stress go much further than skin deep. Literally. When Johan asked us that unexpected question, my first thought was *Why would he ask such an unrelated question? Of course, my marriage is okay,* I reasoned. After all, our major concern is Hennie's return to normality. Our battle lies in his physical recovery from physical loss, but that really wasn't the entire problem. We had to face the battles we were having in our relationship, which had been caused by the severe damage that the trauma brought upon our whole world. We were not so crazy in love any more. We found ourselves to be impatient, irritated and drifting apart.

We knew how to get through the day, to solve problems, and even to respect each other. But those considerations alone did not constitute a thriving marital relationship. The stress had unwittingly spilled over into our relationship. Our view of each other as husband and wife became clouded and even distorted at times. We needed help. We needed time.

Never could I, in a million years, have fathomed the power of time. I still have trouble with understanding this concept. I want to take action, fix it, get results and move on. Now. But I was wrong.

How About You?

The possibility exists that you will never to return to a healthy state of being after the trials and heartache you've been through. If that is part of your story, I don't blame you for it. I have deep empathy with those who don't survive the battles and never really recover. I've met them and I've been privileged to help some, but others were not so easy to assist. Instead of giving themselves more time, they made huge irreversible decisions in very tumultuous situations. Even in those instances, when hearts are ready to submit fully to God, a better future is a sure thing.

Trauma brings loss in your life, loss brings grieving, and grieving takes time. You need to be aware that in the process your relationships are also affected. If your valleys and down times are more frequent than your mountaintops and you have fewer and fewer enjoyable moments in your life, you may be heading for more pain. That which may feel normal for others may be something that can push you to negative behavior and premature decisions. Ending a relationship may not be the answer. Blaming others will not bring better days either. Time. Give yourself time to breathe; give yourself time to heal.

Healing takes time, which is best illustrated in a pathway or cycle of sorts. Knowing this may instill hope within you. Initially, the pain is so constant that it interrupts your life 24/7. As time goes by, you experience moments of freedom from the constant torment of the trauma. After a while, the moments of intense pain and haunting memories will diminish, almost like a cycle that comes around less frequently as time goes by. Finally, you are mostly free, strong enough to deal with the infrequent flashbacks, and your life reaches near normalcy.

The fruit of many years of patience, during which we gave time for healing and allowed room for recovery, brought us to a love that is deeper than we ever thought possible. Fruit takes time to grow. When you can't see anything but sour, undeveloped fruit, take heart and allow time to do its work. You will surely reap a plentiful harvest if you don't give up.

God makes everything beautiful.

In His time.

11

Restored to Beauty

Expecting God to Restore to More Than Before

H ENNIE WAS DOING GREAT—much better than expected. His condition improved daily while he recovered normal function of his
body. He was well on his way to life as close as possible to what it
had been before. Somehow, he was undeterred by his losses, seemingly void of lingering emotional after-effects of the trauma. He was
more than ready to be done with the past and to put the pain behind
him—even with the unanswered questions. Everyone deals differently with trauma, but my husband possesses an incredible inner
resilience to overcome life-altering events. His faith in God is on
another level, which I've witnessed throughout the 35 years we have
been married.

In Unity About Diversity

Hennie and I each had our own battles to fight in getting through
the dark times. One huge difference was that I suffered from after-effects
much more than he did. Because we are all unique, we deal with trauma
differently—even when we have a common faith in God and are each
totally dependent on Him. I wish I could have dealt with the aftermath
like Hennie did, but I did not go through what he went through. I see no
benefit in comparing responses to pain.

In dealing with loss, there is no comparison, but surely there are lessons to learn. Two aspects are important to keep in mind: one person's
loss always affects their loved ones, and God meets us where we are as
we respond to the loss from our own individual experience. I had to deal
with the aftermath according to the way the trauma affected my life and

what it required of me. On the other hand, Hennie was alone in a battle only he could fight.

I have found that when all is said and done, after a long day in the trenches, you are all alone when you lay down your head at night. Alone with God. Alone in your response to your circumstances. When all the noise is gone, each one of us has to take responsibility for our response to pain. Hennie and I had to stay in unity in the fight, yet we were very diverse in how we dealt with it—during the trauma, as well as in the aftermath. How did he cope with the aftermath of this tragedy? I'm so glad you asked!

Hennie's Response

He should be the one writing this book to tell his side of the story! You have probably wondered about that by now. Why isn't he? Simply put, it's not in his nature, nor his desire or conviction to revisit past pain. Maybe it's too much for him to deal with; maybe someday he will, I don't know. We talk about it frequently, since I do believe he has so much to give and so much to say, but for now he does everything in his power to encourage me in our assignment to tell the story. As long as he does not have to sit down for months on end, recalling, reminiscing or figuring out the details of the past, he is content. Writing an autobiography is just not him. It's not in his nature to look back.

My husband is, however, programmed to stand strong and keep moving, while pulling up others who are suffering around him. Do not expect him to linger longer than one moment with you in your pain either. He has a tender heart filled with empathy, yet he does not linger long before guiding you in the way out in very simple terms.

I've often said that if I ever have to be in a foxhole, the only person in the world I would want to be with is my husband. He refuses to camp there, even when I think it's a good idea every now and then to do exactly that. In the heat of the battle, I may think it's time to take a breath, but I'll look around only to find I'm all alone with Hennie way ahead in the distance. When I'm worn out, he keeps going. He is, of course, passionate about the many miracles God has done for him, ready to talk about them with great ease if need be—but only to give the listener a glimpse of God's power to help him keep going.

He has no residual fear, torment or any kind of negative after-effects whatsoever from the traumas in his life. If he had, he'd probably give up and die because he's had more painful experiences than anyone should be required to endure. He may have some scars as a result of tough times, but no angst or hang-ups as might be expected. As a matter of fact, he is the stronger for his trial. If you should ask him why, he'll tell you he learned the power of praise in times of unbearable pain early in life. Too early. He has a powerful testimony of how God infused power into his life through praising God in the midst of the deepest valley. As mentioned in previous chapters, He had been through deep waters even before the burning flames.

My Widower

Before we met, Hennie was married to a beautiful godly woman he loved with all his heart. They were filled with dreams like any other young couple, elated to expect their first baby after a couple years of marriage. She was in the third trimester of a very healthy pregnancy when tragedy suddenly hit. After a vomiting spell, a regular occurrence that plagued her throughout the whole pregnancy, she suffered a massive brain aneurysm that caused instant blindness. She was unconscious by the time they reached the hospital. The medical team placed her on life support while feverishly working to obtain an accurate diagnosis to properly treat her. The decision was made to perform an emergency Caesarean section in an attempt to save the baby's life and to treat any suspected pregnancy complications.

Although she had fallen into a deep coma, the doctors had hope of saving their lives. A beautiful perfectly healthy boy was delivered; unfortunately, vitals quickly deteriorated for both mom and baby. Though the baby was perfect in every way, he was unable to survive because his lungs lacked sufficient intrauterine development. Sadly, both passed away. From a moment of extreme happiness—enjoying the love of a healthy, expectant wife with a child on the way to standing next to two coffins in mere days—how can words describe such grief?

The sudden deaths left their loved ones dumbfounded. Their worlds were destroyed in this horrible turn of events. Hennie suffered compounded loss so insanely abrupt that he was plunged into the depths of despair. How can a person even think in those terms? There is no way. How in the world does a person recover from such tragedy? There are no answers. He was only 23 years of age—a man in mourning much too early in life.

Later in the same year, he relocated to the town where I lived. He was motivated to move there in order to reconnect with our pastor who knew his late wife very well. Our pastor and his wife were wonderful faith-filled people whose hearts were also broken by this tragedy. Hennie was hoping to find comfort with them and to flee the pain by getting far away from where he and his wife had lived. The whole truth is that he had planned to stay in Cape Town only for a while before going backpacking in Europe. He was already prepared with a passport, enough cash, and a backpack filled with traveling essentials. I only learned about the plans much later. The pain was so numbing; the only future he saw for himself was that of a homeless person roaming the streets in Europe.

The pastor's wife was a good friend of mine, and she was also a matchmaker extraordinaire. I remember the first time she told me about Hennie. Her plan was to introduce us to each other, since she thought we would be a perfect match. She had obviously not seen Hennie since his wife died; otherwise, she would have known better. I would not have been interested, simply by his looks! He was a sad pitiful sight with long hair and a long beard and…unfashionable clothing! These were important considerations to me. Forgive me, I was young!

After learning of his tragic story, without any hesitation, I responded with a great big resounding "No!" I was not interested in a man with so much sadness in his past; neither was my dream to live in the shadow of a wonderful woman who once held his heart. It had not been his choice to leave her. He had lost his wife who would remain forever young in his memory, as well as the mother of his first child. Who could compete with that image—by choice? Definitely not me!

I was selfish, young and foolish. I wanted to be the "one and only" of a man who came riding into my life on a white horse, snatching me away from the doom of a lifetime of loneliness. I had to be the answer to his dreams; he had to be my hero and handsome as well, of course. That was my plan—until I met Hennie at church one Sunday. He was about to derail my carefully crafted schemes about how my life was going to play out.

Even after we had talked at church several times, there was no chemistry for me at all. That all changed after a haircut and one date—a haircut I gave him and a date as a sign of his appreciation. It all started when he asked me to cut his difficult-to-manage hair after learning I was in the hair business. I'm always up for a challenge, so I agreed to show him a thing or two about my skills with any kind of hair. The night of the haircut, I had a close friend with me so as not to be alone with him.

After he left, though, my friend took one look at me and realized there was something going on—something more than a haircut. There was. I discovered this wonderful person underneath the misleading exterior. He was smart, kind, caring, and of course, drop-dead handsome! I refused payment for the haircut, but happily accepted the invite for a milkshake instead. That became our official first of lifetime of dates to follow. *How did this wonderfully handsome man hide so well under all that hair?* And the clothes…the rest is history!

I found in him a man who knew how to appreciate love because he had known and lost great love. I found a man who, more than most others, appreciated togetherness with the ones he loves because he has tasted the wonder of it and lost it all. I loved his quiet strength and how he never boasted of what he had or knew; instead, he was secure in who he was, unmoved by people's opinions. He was that man—the one with whom I fell head over heels in love, and he still is that man today. I got to marry the love of my life. That is not a given for everyone, so I don't take it lightly. I am beyond grateful.

None of my fears of marrying a widower came true; on the contrary, no one could have loved me more or better. I have never felt second-best; rather, I learned a lot about respect. He honored me enough to allow me to be exactly who I was. I never was burdened with a heavy load of expectations, but lovingly encouraged and given room to grow. What more could I have asked for?

Rendezvous with God

How was Hennie able to love again after such great loss? This story is one he should also tell, but because he is not going to—at least not in this book, I will. He had a supernatural experience with God that dislodged the first brick in a wall of pain that surrounded him. That experience initiated a process of healing when, in that moment, he felt comfort for the first time since he buried his wife and son. The course of his life was changed when God started putting his heart back together so he could trust it with someone else again.

Somewhere along the way on his drive to Cape Town during his move, he stopped to take a break by one of the most beautiful nature scenes he loved so much. The beauty of the landscape was astounding and the silence deafening as he brought his broken heart before God one more time. God began to speak to him about the intricacies of each and every little wildflower around him, how it was not by chance but by His design that every detail was carefully preserved for him to enjoy. It was as if he'd never seen it before—as if a revelation of the perfection of creation suddenly baffled him. He picked a flower, took a closer look and stared at its perfection in total amazement. Everything about it was wonderfully created. The flower did not deserve nor contribute but had been created and sustained by God's love.

In that moment, God made it clear to Hennie that He was doing the same with him. He cared about the most personal details of his life just as He did for the flower. The same way He had expressed Himself through the beauty of creation, He promised to do in Hennie's life. There was hope; the Creator had stepped in.

God revealed to Hennie that day that He was acquainted with the pain in each piece of his broken heart—just as He knew each detail of the wildflower. Hennie started thanking God for the beauty in the flower, as well as His presence in all of nature. Before he knew it, thanking God turned into praising Him, which momentarily caused the unbearable weight of grief to lift from his heart. Hennie did not expect what was happening to him, but he felt the warm, comforting love of God surrounding him as if he were immersed in the vastness of God's affection toward him. That one touch from heaven, that one word from God, the unexpected awe of the love of God changed something in his heart. There God started "heart surgery" to restore unspeakable brokenness so Hennie could love again. The restoration was a process from then on, but one moment in the presence of God changed his life forever.

This is a story I understand better the longer I know Hennie. First of all, he has a godly connection to nature where he feels closest to God and where he experiences calm like nowhere else. Second, once God speaks, that settles the matter for him. Once he hears from God, nothing else is necessary. God, in His great mercy, met Hennie at his point of desperate need through nature that day. That meeting empowered him to continue in full faith that God was well able to carry him where he never thought he could walk. By miraculous intervention, God taught Hennie how to deal with trauma. None of it was easy, but pure grace supernaturally poured into his heart.

The Power of Praise

At the time of the burn, he already knew the power of praising God and how praise had kept him breathing when his heart was in shreds. It was as if he was on autopilot after the burn accident, which caused him to praise God spontaneously during the worst pain. His praising was something everyone marveled about, but it was nothing new for Hennie. He knew the power in praise. He had experienced it. Praise became a lifestyle for him, especially during difficult times. Those who know Hennie will now understand why his favorite saying is "Praise God." Seriously, he says it whether or not it's fitting, and whether or not others think it's fitting.

Over the many years since the accident, God has restored beauty to us in too many ways to recount. I believe it is one of the reasons we get to tell our story thirty years later. From the vantage point of looking back over a lifetime of living in the abundance of God's blessings in our lives, we can see more clearly how God worked all things together for good. Ours is not an overnight recovery story, but one of God's faithfulness over a long trying period. Judging God in the heat of the moment can be so easy, but passing judgment often leads to erroneous assumptions about life, love, and the goodness of God.

Hennie was left with lost dreams, a shattered heart, empty arms, a broken body, and a dim future, but God restored it all into a full healthy life marked by love and adventure. He once was sick; now he is well. He once stood at a dark grave; now he remembers that time as a beautiful love he shared for a while. He once was lost in despair; now he brings hope to others. We once were aliens in a foreign land; now we proudly salute the colors. We once depended on the goodness of others; now we are called to take it back to them. We once were two who became one. Before we knew it, we were five when our three kids came into our lives. Now we are nine, since God added four more boys! There is Matthew, our gift from heaven who married Yolandie, and our grandsons Wyatt, Wesley and Walter. Love multiplied into the new lives who walked into our world. How can we in a million years recount the goodness of God?

Restores to More

Ours was not at all an easy road void of challenges, but we have lived it long enough to know that in the end, God restores to more. Restoration is simply His nature. It may take time, it may take a journey, but it will always remain true. Scripture is filled with examples meant to teach us the attributes of God: God is good; He is big; He creates, gives, multiplies and restores.

The Widow and Her Son

Who in the world walks up to a widow and asks her for her last piece of bread? She had enough food for one more meal for her and her son before they were going to starve to death. She even admitted that they were going to eat one more meal, then die. A prophet of God was asking for her bread. He told her to go make the bread, then bring him the first piece. Unbelievable! Elijah told her that if she did what he asked, she would have food during the drought until the rain came again. As a result of her obedience to give him the last bit of what she had, she had food to eat beyond her own supply, as well as miraculous provision during the famine.

This widow suffered lack before her encounter with God through the prophet; she experienced abundance after God restored her supply. She would have sold herself short if she had not acted in faith. Instead of being "exactly like before," she experienced God's "more than before."

In her case, it came through obedience and learning that in giving you prepare to receive. She didn't think she had anything to give, but the fact is, everyone has something to give—even if it is a button off your shirt. Generosity, though it seemingly makes no sense at all, is released over your life when you give, especially in obedience to God.

We need to see with the eyes of faith the storehouse of God, which sometimes only happens when you give away your last piece of bread. In the times of your deepest need, it may take an additional step of faith to line up with the plan of God for your life. Take that step because when God restores, it is always to more than before.

The Sad Man Covered in Ashes

With friends like his, who needed enemies? His wife hated his breath; his own kids looked down on him as his livelihood vanished into thin air. He became an absolute disgrace to all who saw him. This man was the epitome of a fall from grace. In an attempt to help him, the only counsel his friends could offer amounted to long sermons of how sin had caused all his misfortune. They found the answers to Job's problems, which, in fact, offered more questions than answers. They insisted that his problem was sin, so he had to repent in order for his disastrous life to be restored.

The man was a mess! There was no way anyone could understand how a righteous man, with extreme wealth such as his, had ended up on a heap of ashes. He sat in total despair, ready to die, scratching his own infested body like a diseased, deserted animal. He once was very rich, known for his wealth and faith in God—known on earth, as well as in heaven.

The Bible says Satan challenged God about Job. He told God that Job's prosperity was tied to his righteousness, and he declared that if he should lose all of his wealth, he would no longer serve God. God gave Satan permission to destroy all Job had, except his life. Consequently, he suffered the terrible loss of his children, his livestock, his health, and the support of his wife. After plunging as far down as possible without physically dying, Job ended up cursing the day he was born. Job's is a fascinating story, worthy of being read again.

Job never cursed God as his wife suggested, and it never was sin that brought him so low. While he endured the public scorn, the judgment of his so-called friends, the loss of his family and livelihood, and the repulsive infestation of disease in his body, God was acutely aware of every detail.

God even entered into a discussion with Job where he was out of words, having experienced the powerful presence of God. His self-righteous discourse turned into prayers for his friends when he was one step away from death. Job never once deserted God. On the contrary, he asserted that even if God were to slay him, he would still trust Him. Job could have descended no lower, except the grave, when God intervened and turned his life around. By the hand of God, Job was restored to twice what he had before his loss—redeemed to more than before.

This illustration does not mean that everyone going through trials does so for the same reason Job did. It does, though, give us a glimpse into the unseen world, revealing there is always more to a situation than our eyes can see. Job was a righteous man when he was rich, as well as when he was worth less than a sick dog. He had to realize that even his righteousness was not enough to move God's hand, and he had to refrain from rehearsing his own uprightness. When there was no more to say and no understanding to be found, God spoke. Job said that he had believed God all his life, but this time he saw God with his own eyes. He came face to face with his Creator, where there was no recourse or earthly reasoning, only submission. When Job was humbled to the point of praying for his judgmental friends, God found his heart ready to be restored.

The Little Boy's Lunch

Jesus and His friends must have been tired. They had been busy all day long praying for sick people to be healed. The mission was so successful that huge crowds of people followed them wherever they went. They had never seen anything like that in their entire lives. People who had been deathly sick were suddenly healthy! Word spread quickly, which increased the crowds of needy and noisy people. The followers were so desperate that even when it grew late, not one of the 5,000 of them wanted to go home.

Jesus looked at the masses of people and felt sorry for them. They acted like a bunch of sheep who had lost their way and were getting very hungry. So He told His disciples to give them food. The disciples were flabbergasted that Jesus would make such a request, since feeding all of them would be impossible. Even if they had the money, there was no baker with enough bread for everyone. One little boy in the crowd had not yet eaten the lunch his mother must have packed. At least someone was thinking ahead! However, he only had enough for one little boy to eat. The disciples brought his five loaves and two fish to Jesus as evidence of the impossibility of the situation. It was ridiculously laughable to assume that one little boy's lunch could feed such a huge crowd.

But Jesus took the small lunch, accepting it as seed for what He was about to do. All Jesus needed was just a seed—a shadow of a miracle to grow into enough to meet the demand. The five loaves and two fish were not enough for food, but were enough for seed—only because Jesus was there. Jesus took it, gave thanks, and broke it. He proceeded to hand it to the disciples to give to the people. Somewhere in the handing of the morsels from one hand to the next, it became more, increasing so much that even after everyone had eaten, there were leftovers everywhere. Jesus told the disciples to gather the crumbs the hungry crowd had left behind. They gathered twelve baskets filled with bread! Why could Jesus not have increased the food to just enough? The situation was impossible to begin with! The crowds were hungry, desperate for a miracle, until God stepped in with provision beyond their wildest expectations. It's as if God can't do anything in moderation! Look what happened when He created humans—brilliant creatures not even capable of using all of the brainpower that was given. Above and beyond, that is where God lives.

I identify with that characteristic as a mother. I find it impossible to cook just enough food. Even now that my kids are adults, I still cook as if I have a house full of hungry people. It's to the point where I have become the laughing stock of my family as the one who is incapable of making small amounts of food. God is exactly like that. He does not operate in the realm of less! Most of us do, however. We are trapped by our own minds by what is possible in our own understanding. Yet God invites us to live by faith in what we can't see. The question is not "What can you see?" but rather, "What can you believe?" How awesome is that! How much are we missing? How limited are we? How limitless is God?

So What? In Each Instance...

◆ **The Persons Involved Had to Answer a Call.**

Job had to refrain from cursing God. He had to remain loyal to God, righteous whether in sackcloth and ashes, or when he was a wealthy businessman. He lost all— except his faith in God.

The widow was called to trust God with her very last morsel of food—the very crumbs life had thrown to her. She had to decide whether to walk out on a limb with God or cling to what she could see. Once she chose, her miracle was unleashed.

The disciples had to act out in public what could have been their greatest moments of utter foolishness. They instructed the people to sit in groups, while there was nothing close to meeting the need. They were willing to become part of an operation, a huge endeavor, which was doomed to failure before it even started. In the physical realm, feeding the 5,000 surely was nothing short of a disaster, but because they were willing to take action, they felt the bread multiply in their own hands.

♦ **Heaven Touched Earth.**

The unseen power of God manifested in the seen world. The spiritual became physical. The impossible manifested. There was a transfer from the resources of God to fill the lack of His people. There was a need that turned into more provision than what was needed. The miracles did not heap provision on them for the rest of their lives. They still had to go home where other issues required miracles as well. It didn't mean all of life was now perfect. The crowds had to eat again. The widow needed another miracle when her son became deathly ill. Job reared another family and ran his restored business, which surely presented new challenges.

♦ **God's Intention Is Not to Do Life for Us.**

He is not in the business of making us comfortable. He shows us His great power as monumental reminders of who we are as His children. His desire is to build our faith, develop our character and help us mature, so we know we are not a bunch of wandering sheep but children of the Most High God. He reveals His character to us so we can grow in our love for Him, respond to His sacrifice for us, live by faith, and know what He says is true.

God Is Not Surprised

In our personal lives, Hennie and I are in faith for many things we have not seen. God has done so much, and He has shown Himself to us so many times, yet we still stand in faith for what we believe God has planned for our future. I know it's the same with you. God is not upset at you. You have not disappointed Him, for He knows everything even before it happens. He is not surprised by your circumstances, but in great mercy He wants to raise you up. We only see in the natural, and by faith, we can even see our needs met, but what God sees is beyond all we see to a place of more-than-enough.

May His peace, His goodness, and His comfort overshadow your heart to a supply of more than enough, so you can freely give to others without running out!

The Lord is my light and my salvation; Whom shall I fear? The Lord is the strength of my life; Of whom shall I be afraid?

When the wicked came against me To eat up my flesh, My enemies and foes, They stumbled and fell.

Though an army may encamp against me, My heart shall not fear; Though war may rise against me, In this I will be confident.

One thing I have desired of the Lord, That will I seek: That I may dwell in the house of the Lord All the days of my life, To behold the beauty of the Lord, And to inquire in His temple.

For in the time of trouble He shall hide me in His pavilion; In the secret place of His tabernacle He shall hide me; He shall set me high upon a rock.

And now my head shall be lifted up above my enemies all around me; Therefore I will offer sacrifices of joy in His tabernacle; I will sing, yes, I will sing praises to the LORD. *Hear, O* LORD, *when I cry with my voice! Have mercy also upon me, and answer me.*

When You said, "Seek My face," My heart said to You, "Your face, LORD, *I will seek."*

Do not hide Your face from me; Do not turn Your servant away in anger; You have been my help; Do not leave me nor forsake me, O God of my salvation.

When my father and my mother forsake me, Then the LORD *will take care of me.*

Teach me Your way, O LORD, *And lead me in a smooth path, because of my enemies.*

Do not deliver me to the will of my adversaries; For false witnesses have risen against me, And such as breathe out violence.

I would have lost heart, unless I had believed That I would see the goodness of the LORD *In the land of the living.*

Wait on the LORD; *Be of good courage, And He shall strengthen your heart; Wait, I say, on the* LORD! (Psalm 27)

12

Hold Your Ground (Part I)

Staying Alive and Thriving When Trouble Hits

O NE DAY, I AWOKE around 4:00 a.m., disturbed by the sound of dripping. I lay there listening, wondering whether the noise came from the inside or the outside; after all, a soft rain was falling. The more cognizant I became, the more I realized we might have a problem on our hands. We were sleeping in our motorhome next to the ocean. *Oh no, please tell me the roof is not leaking!*

I woke Hennie, hoping against hope that he would assure me the sound was outside, but it was not to be. We sat up in bed only to see the rain dripping from the roof vent right above our bed. Certainly not a fun way to wake up, but thank God, I did wake up before the problem worsened. Hennie quickly fixed the rain's point of entry—in perfect character for "Mr. Fix-It-All."

Of course, the more practical action would have been to fix the slight crack in the vent cap the first time "Mr. Fix-It-All" noticed it. The weather was great at the time, posing very little danger that we would get wet from a leak. The minor imperfection was put on hold until later. Later was okay, but it should have been done before the next rain!

We started our day by scrambling to stop the leak and fixing the crack, instead of enjoying our usual early morning coffee. I would have much rather been awakened by the sound of the waves, before slowly making my way to the kitchen where Hennie had our two cups of delicious java waiting on the table. Funny how the crack in the vent cap was of absolutely no concern...until the rain came.

203

Set for Success

It is often the same in life. Obviously, being well-prepared, having no cracks in the vent, ready to be safe and dry no matter what the weather outside is the better way to live! There are ways to live, actions to take, decisions to make, and wisdom to apply, which will make all the difference when tragedy strikes.

Life lessons can be learned in one of two ways: gleaning wisdom from other people's experience, or by our own experience. I recommend the former though it's not always possible; it is preferable if you have a choice. There are many ways in which to live with wisdom and to be in close relationship with God in troubled times.

The tighter the body and the stronger the core of an athlete, the greater his balance and resistance will be. The best way to meet any obstacle or resistance in athletics is to be strong for the challenge. A non-athlete can surely enter any race, but he will falter sooner, drag along slower, require help from fellow competitors, or even quit. It is the same spiritually. When the going gets tough, it is always best to be battle-ready beforehand, armed with provisions that will sustain you and keep you alive.

There are ways to position yourself in life in order not to fall apart when trouble hits, to have knowledge and wisdom to consider when circumstances get out of control. Making preparation for tough times when things are going well is far better than being found weak when life hurts. Ponder the condition of the following stabilizers in your life as this is how to remain strong and steady when all hell breaks loose.

How to Stay Alive and Thrive When Trouble Hits

1. Be Rightly Related with God at All Times

In Good Times

When our worst day unexpectedly shows up, being in a healthy place with God sets us up for more resilience and endurance. To find God in troubled times is not impossible, but God has much value to add to your life when life is good as well as when life brings serious challenges.

Good times are much more detrimental to our walk with God than bad times. Faking commitment when all is well is easy, and that's a dangerous place to be because it's not real commitment; rather, it's a disappointment waiting to happen. Selfishness festers in conditions void of trouble or stress—much like a child gets spoiled for reality when needs are offered on a silver platter every day. This is a sad truth to learn because we all would rather live in the bliss of easy street.

The paradox in life is that who you really are during good times will become public during bad times. Good times should not be without strength training, which can only happen intentionally through discipline. When there is no pressure, the wise person applies discipline to bring the resistance that causes strength to grow. I do believe this is part of the explanation of why God allows us to go through trouble; for without resistance we regress in selfish weakness to a self-created world where "I" is king. In that world we have no use for God, a condition that puts us on a road to eternal damnation.

Even in everyday life issues, such as our careers, health, relationships, etc., healthy exercise in character development will produce much greater success. In good times we should develop self-imposed good morals and high standards that demand discipline, healthy habits, and the observance of beautiful traditions and rules of decency.

Such a lifestyle in good times will serve us well when we encounter bad times.

We should seek God with all our hearts when times are good. We should follow habits, such as Bible study, prayer and meditation, and practical daily service, that will help us to know God better. Then when times turn from good to bad, we will have a strong foundation during the storm. Be disciplined to make God a conscious and vital part of your daily life, and you will enjoy the benefits of a life sustained by His presence and power.

The Israelites provide a good example of the danger of regressing during the good times. We read in Scripture how they fell away from God while they enjoyed prosperity. They started serving other gods, marrying foreign women, and indulging in many sinful practices. Their hearts grew calloused toward God. Time and time again God allowed their enemies to overcome them so that they would repent and turn back to Him. They were clearly on a path of destruction, drowning in their own pleasures in times of peace.

When Moses was on the mountain receiving the law from God, the people below began to indulge in sinful merrymaking. They lost sight of the discipline and rules of conduct, which resulted in an orgy that brought deadly consequences. This episode serves as a stark warning for all of us to stay close to God in good times. Live in a state of gratitude, never forgetting who our Provider is!

In Bad Times

Private faith becomes public when we experience bad times. Bad times reveal:

- **The Level of Commitment**
  Three Hebrew boys were ready to face a blazing furnace rather than bow down to the gold image that King Nebuchadnezzar had ordered

everyone to worship. They were undeterred in their commitment to God, even facing a hideous death by fire. The three bound men, joined by a fourth man, freely walked around in the oven, unscathed by the fire and not even smelling like smoke when they came out! The king's words:

> *"Look!" he answered, "I see four men loose, walking in the midst of the fire; and they are not hurt, and the form of the fourth is like the Son of God." (Daniel 3:25)*

God saved them inside the fire! He could have prevented them from going into the fire, but their trial meant a walk inside the fire. As a result, the king decreed that there is no God other than the God in the fire. The level of commitment of these three men was void of any reservation or limits whatsoever. That commitment showed when the heat was on. It is the same with all of us today.

♦ **Superficial Faith**

The faith of Ananias and Sapphira was determined by what was in their purse. Prior to their lucrative real estate transaction, their level of faith was assumed to be deep, like all of the other believers. According to Acts 5, once they had the money in their pockets, they lied about their profits thinking that no one would ever know. Because of their deceit, they were struck dead. How incredibly sad are the consequences of lying to God, pretending to be more committed than what we really are.

♦ **The Need to Impress People Rather Than God**

King Saul crafted his own destruction when he allowed his fame, coupled with the adoration of the people, to become his god. What a sad, unfortunate ending of unlimited potential!

> *Then Saul said to Samuel, "I have sinned, for I have transgressed the commandment of the LORD and your words, because I feared*

the people and obeyed their voice. Now therefore, please pardon my sin, and return with me, that I may worship the LORD." But Samuel said to Saul, "I will not return with you, for you have rejected the word of the LORD, and the LORD has rejected you from being king over Israel." (1 Samuel 15:24-26)

We all face a challenge when our public image is at stake, so let's not judge Saul so readily. He enjoyed extensive power with high approval ratings from the people, but he tried to walk on both sides of the fence. With God, it is all or nothing. Lukewarmness is repulsive to Him.

♦ **Ulterior Motives**

Judas sat at the table during the Last Supper with Jesus the night that He was to be betrayed. He was not a part of the unity this meal signified because he was bound up by greed and had already conspired to betray Jesus. Who would suspect that one of their own would strike the fatal blow that sent Jesus to the cross?

Then one of the twelve, called Judas Iscariot, went to the chief priests and said, "What are you willing to give me if I deliver Him to you?" And they counted out to him thirty pieces of silver. So from that time he sought opportunity to betray Him.

(Matthew 26:14-16)

♦ **Whom We Fear Most**

When the Israelites were standing on the threshold of the Promised Land, only two of the twelve spies were ready to take God at His word and drive out the giants who occupied the land God had given to them. Two men stood in the face of the giants, but sadly, they were a minority. The people feared the opposition, and as a result, they wandered in the desert for forty more years. Their trust fell short when it was time to put it into action. The promise was in front of them, yet they lacked the faith to overcome the one last obstacle between them and their land. Their fear of the giants revealed the level of their faith. Their failure is too sad for words. Once again, it's easy to judge; yet how often do we profess our great faith, only until we see the size of the "giants" guarding our promise?

We need to be close to God at all times. While we have the opportunity, God wants to give us abundant life in both good and bad times. For our own sakes, seeking God while there is light shows wisdom, yet there is no bad time when we cannot get closer to God! Even when it seems too late, it never is—even when we have failed God.

2. Use Your Sword; It's a Fight

Tension is a constant in life. There are two opposing kingdoms at play on earth: the kingdom of God and the kingdom of darkness. The world is under the influence of the kingdom of darkness, the sway of Lucifer. He is called *the god of this age* in 2 Corinthians 4:4, *the prince of the power of the air* in Ephesians 2:2, and *the ruler of this world* in John 12:31.

Two opposing kingdoms are currently at work on earth. Satan has spiritual power in which God has allowed him to operate on earth since the fall of man in Genesis. The kingdom of God is supreme and all-powerful through the blood of Jesus that was shed on the cross on earth. Therefore, Satan's power is always subject to the kingdom and power of God on earth and can only function wherever God allows.

God won the battle when His Son died on the cross, yet Satan still has rule over this world system where the blood of Jesus does not oppose. We are not called to change the way the kingdoms on earth operate. That is under God's control, but we are called to be catalysts for the change, to usher in the kingdom of God wherever we live. We are the body of Christ on earth, so we carry with us the redemptive influence and power of the blood of Jesus Christ. God has chosen to establish His kingdom on earth through the redeemed followers of Christ. We, therefore, operate in the tension created by two opposing kingdoms: the kingdom of God through the power of Christ in us, and the kingdom of darkness that operates in designated power. There is constant resistance and tension that causes a battle for which we should dress!

The fight is for the soul of man: your soul, your life, my soul and my life. The mere fact that we are residents on earth, even as redeemed by Christ, does not shelter us from demonic influences, including any kind of sickness or sorrow, but Satan cannot touch our redeemed souls. He tempts us to hand our soul to him, like he did with Jesus in the desert, but he can't simply take it. Once we are under the blood of Jesus Christ, even with our flesh subject to evil systems on earth, we function in the kingdom of God where we are protected.

As followers of Christ, we qualify for the benefits of the kingdom of God, but we have to enforce our rights to them since we live in a fallen world. This is what the Bible refers to as "the war," "the fight," "the race," or "the battle."

God has given us battle gear, i.e., spiritual clothes we can wear and spiritual weapons we should use. When we choose not to use them, we are rendered weak and defeated, even as believers with rights to the benefits of the kingdom of God.

Though we walk in the flesh, we do not war according to the flesh. For the weapons of our warfare are not carnal but mighty in God for pulling down strongholds. (2 Corinthians 10:3-4)

God provided armor for our war, including a sword. The sword is called "the sword of the Spirit" (the Word of God). The Bible contains our rights and privileges, which we fight for by believing and speaking the will of God for our lives.

In times of trial or pain, what is your protection?

- "Everyone is against me. If only I could get away."
- "My spouse will get me out of this."

- "I'm educated."
- "I deserve better."
- "I'll go to church on Sunday."
- "I'm a good person."

These notions may temporarily solve some battles, but I have found them weak in helping me when I am in pain. A fight requires a sword, not excuses.

In times of trials or pain, how do you respond?

- With uncontrolled anger to arouse fear in others in order to get your way?
- With insults, accusations, telling people off, diminishing the value of others in order to be superior or in control?
- With tearing up, playing the victim, evoking pity in order to get your way regardless of your own actions?
- With ignoring others, withdrawing, displaying aggression in a passive way in order to manipulate or enforce your superiority?

It is a losing battle that settles nothing, but only causes a pause until the next outburst of the same. A recurring cycle of anything that does not work is evidence of an incorrect diagnosis or treatment! We have to identify who our real enemy is and fight with the appropriate weapons.

Take up the Word of God to refute the lies of the ruler of this world with the sword of the Spirit. Add the following verses to your arsenal, for this is the will of God for you:

Direct my steps by Your word, and let no iniquity have dominion over me. (Psalm 119:133)

Behold, children are a heritage from the LORD, the fruit of the womb is a reward. (Psalm 127:3)

The LORD shall preserve you from all evil; He shall preserve your soul. The LORD shall preserve your going out and your coming in from this time forth, and even forevermore. (Psalm 121:7-8)

But He was wounded for our transgressions, He was bruised for our iniquities; the chastisement for our peace was upon Him, and by His stripes we are healed. (Isaiah 53:5)

The Spirit of the Lord GOD is upon Me, because the Lord has anointed Me to preach good tidings to the poor; He has sent Me to heal the brokenhearted, to proclaim liberty to the captives, and the opening of the prison to those who are bound. (Isaiah 61:1)

And we know that all things work together for good to those who love God, to those who are the called according to His purpose.
(Romans 8:28)

If God is for us, who can be against us? He who did not spare His own Son, but delivered Him up for us all, how shall He not with Him also freely give us all things? (Romans 8:31-32)

For I am persuaded that neither death nor life, nor angels nor principalities nor powers, nor things present nor things to come, nor height nor depth, nor any other created thing, shall be able to separate us from the love of God which is in Christ Jesus our Lord. (Romans 8:38-39)

God is faithful, who will not allow you to be tempted beyond what you are able, but with the temptation will also make the way of escape, that you may be able to bear it. (1 Corinthians 10:12)

My grace is sufficient for you, for My strength is made perfect in weakness. (2 Corinthians 12:9)

He who has begun a good work in you will complete it until the day of Jesus Christ. (Philippians 1:6)

Be anxious for nothing, but in everything by prayer and supplication, with thanksgiving, let your requests be made known to God; and the peace of God, which surpasses all understanding, will guard your hearts and minds through Christ Jesus. (Philippians 4:6-7)

I can do all things through Christ who strengthens me.
(Philippians 4:13)

Jesus Christ is the same yesterday, today, and forever.
(Hebrews 13:8)

If we are faithless, He remains faithful; He cannot deny Himself.
(2 Timothy 2:13)

My son, do not forget my law, but let your heart keep my commands; for length of days and long life and peace they will add to you.
(Proverbs 3:1-2)

Trust in the LORD with all your heart, and lean not on your own understanding; in all your ways acknowledge Him, and He shall direct your paths. (Proverbs 3:5-6)

3. Stand in Your Spot

Several years ago when I was part of a small group discussion, we were asked to relate the one thing we remembered about our mothers that had made an impact on our lives. After pondering a moment, I saw my mother in my mind's eye and gave this clear answer: "She filled her spot." Or as the answer came to me in my mother tongue: "Sy het haar plek vol gestaan."

The other members around the table were struck by the poignancy of what I had said, so "standing in your spot" became a saying in our circles.

My mother taught me countless lessons—the obvious ones when I was little, and the teach-by-example ones as I grew older. To even begin singing her praises would require a whole book, as she was truly remarkable by the standards of everyone who knew her. Heaven was made richer when she arrived, and earth was left poorer the day she left.

I have found standing in my spot has served me well in life. Adopting that little sentiment saved me from messing up my life, it helped me to realize and stay true to my calling, and it enabled me to serve as an example to my own children.

My Mother

Please allow me to include excerpts from the note of remembrance I wrote after her passing:

> My mother was a quiet, loyal, tender, yet very strong person. She was a real lady who believed in routine. Neither demanding nor difficult to get along with, she humbled herself rather than create drama. She was the most hardworking woman I've ever known, skillful in everything from cooking jam to sewing clothes, tending a beautiful garden, and more things than I can mention.

> When she put her mind to do something, nothing stood in her way. The kitchen was easily turned into a production facility when it was time to cook melon jam or bake for the bake sale at church. Before dinner everything was back in place with dinner ready on the table. We never missed a meal or wondered whether we had anything to wear or eat. Laundry done, car washed, nails manicured, hair done, and on and on. Through routine she was able to keep up. She made a plan and worked it out.

> She was without doubt a superb dressmaker, and her own hands made most of her clothes. Every single piece of the ones

she didn't make were altered for a better fit. She loved working with her hands. She knitted all her own sweaters and even sewed designer jackets. She loved fabric and yarn; she probably had enough for a store! Her home and her appearance were kept meticulously. When the doorbell rang—before the days of call or text, so yes, friends just showed up—she'd turn on the kettle before sitting down to visit. Tea, never without her homemade cookies neatly on a tray with doilies, created countless favorite memories.

My dad was crazy about her. Sometimes he'd stare at her, ready to compliment her on her appearance and style. They were married for 53 years before he went to be with the Lord. The greatest joy in his life was to brag about her, to buy her perfume and to make sure she always had her favorite chocolate stashed somewhere.

She was on the "Dorcas Committee," the benevolence committee of our church, regularly visiting the elderly, sick, widows, etc., and taking an active part in fundraising for orphanages among other benevolent organizations our church supported. Not a month went by without her tithe, missions offering and building fund contribution in the offering basket. That was first on her little budget outline she kept in the drawer.

She sang in the church choir, loved to read and talk about the end times, enjoyed sitting in the afternoon sun, washed everything that could be washed…and not washed, forever painting something that needed to be spruced up. She loved to travel; boy, did she love to travel. My dad as well. On the countless trips they made to visit us from South Africa, my dad was frequently singled out at the airport for a thorough search. I believe it was because he looked like a mix between a mafia boss and an Irish gentleman—sure to catch security's attention with his sports jacket and cream hat. Yes, even on those long international trips—Mom was right alongside him—pantyhose, high heels, done hair and all.

She never gossiped. I still cannot figure that one out—never had a need to talk about anyone in a negative way. We never had roasted pastor for Sunday lunch either; since she had been reared in a pastor's house, she knew how that went. She lived to be 90 years old, which was way too short for a saint such as she. I can go on and on, but will conclude with this: she filled her spot.

How About You?

Stand in your spot and run in your lane because you have been wonderfully and fearfully created for a particular purpose. Don't compare yourself with or strive to be someone else. You will defeat the whole purpose of your unique design. There is no one else like you on earth—no one! Trying to be someone else must be terribly exhausting! It's like walking with a shoe that doesn't fit or like David of old trying out Saul's armor for a fight. It didn't work; he could hardly move!

Be your unique you. The world needs you to be exactly who you are created to be. We all definitely need to grow, but the growth is to be into more of who we are. Maybe the end result will be a better version of ourselves. But don't try to be a copy of someone who already exists! You are perfectly created with all the potential you need to find your spot. Find it, live it, enjoy it!

My Dad

Since I am giving honor to my mother's memory in this chapter, please allow me also to give you a glimpse of a wonderful man I loved with all my heart—my dad.

He was no different; he filled his spot with greatness, frequently under very difficult circumstances. I miss my mom more than I can say in words, but more than a decade after he went to be with the Lord, the thought of my dad not here with me makes me cry. He left a void in my heart that no one else on earth can fill. I'm comforted, yet miss him still.

Two years after his passing, I wrote a short piece to him on Father's Day that may be most fitting to include. During my quiet time with God, with a very sad heart, I pondered what it was that I missed the most about him. The following thoughts came to me:

Dad,

If I have to pick a part of you that affected me most, it has to be your hands. The signs of what you have done for me were on your hands. I loved your hands. They brought comfort to me. I sometimes stared at them, examined them, and got to know some of what was in your heart that way. It was a paradox in a way since they were rough with hard callouses at times, but so handsome, so hardworking, bringing great security to my young life. They were especially handsome when you wore those rings, when you were all dressed up and ready to go out. What a dresser you were! Coordinated in color and style, zero wrinkles, perfectly fitting, and appropriate in every way.

I knew it was with those hands that you earned each cent that took care of me. With heavy tools in cold and heat, they never tried to pamper themselves, but provided instead the home I loved. How many times those fingers got in the way I can hardly count. That thumb was the one I felt most sorry for! It often was purple and bruised, yet accompanied by no more complaining beyond that one first power word that might have been spoken the second it suffered the injury.

I knew though, for as long as those hands were around, I

was safe. Without a doubt they would stop any harm that might come my way. I saw how they stopped spoil from settling in my brothers' hearts when they warmed up their behinds! Yes, it made me fearful at times but taught me to fear God, teaching me boundaries that served me well when you were no longer there to protect me.

Those hands stopped their toil on earth, but my comfort rests in knowing two truths that are still alive in my heart. First, they must be of great help up there in heaven with God, preparing for the feast. Second, here on earth with me are still two hands that comfort, protect and guide me. It is also my favorite part about Jesus if I had to pick—His two nail-scarred hands.

13

Hold Your Ground (Part II)

Evaluating the Roles of People and Seasons in Your Life

I N the previous chapter, the first three ways to remain stable in troubled times were addressed. First, we need to stay rightly related with God in both the good and the bad times. Second, we need to take up our sword and fight since we are in a battle. Third, each one of us has our own spot to fill, which is crucial to remember when the troubles hit. We so easily question God, retreat from the fight, or forget who we are.

Let's consider two additional, more introspective, issues which are also essential in our walk through pain:

4. The People Factor

People in our lives are crucial to the outcome of our future, especially when we are in the midst of trials. We are more vulnerable to influences; therefore, we should be careful who speaks into our lives when we are down.

Discernment in the roles people play in our lives can be very difficult to attain. It is subjective even in good times, and all the more so in painful emotional times. God places specific people in our lives, so we should carefully give attention to those who cross our path. But not everyone who walks into our lives should be given the power to influence.

The wrong people in the wrong roles in our lives can rob us of the promises of God, or lead us where we should not go. It may seem right at the time, and it may even feel good, but it may not necessarily be God's will for our lives. Staying close with God and hearing from Him about people in our lives will always be the best way to develop friendships. Pray and ask God to close and open doors, to make it clear whether or not certain people should stay in your life. There is wisdom to be had about the people in our lives which may help clear the air or bring peace to our hearts.

Every person in our lives will fit into one of the categories that follow. What is written is not meant to defame or dishonor people; rather, my intent is to lead to more clarity in whom to trust, explain the reason for past pain in relationships, and to bring a touch of logic in a mostly emotional decision or understanding.

People Come into Your Life

- ◆ For a reason
- ◆ For a season
- ◆ Forever
- ◆ For never

For-a-Reason People

- ▶ The roles are one-sided or going both ways, i.e., they are there for you, and you are there for them. You are both called into each other's lives *for a reason.*
- ▶ The roles may only become clear after a while, but their impact on your life will last a lifetime.
- ▶ They are meant to teach, form, influence, or even love you for a reason, uniquely connected to you for a purpose.
- ▶ The connection may end or it may last; you will be forever changed in a positive way as a result of the connection.
- ▶ These could initially be problematic, demanding, or painful relationships, professional or personal. You may not have a

choice in the matter or may simply know they are there to refine you—to even be your teacher. They may be the rock in your shoe God uses to get you to change shoes, but something good will eventually come from it. If you endure, you will look back and realize the significance for the rest of your life.

A Healthy Response
- It was meant to be, whether it was painful or blissful.
- If it's not meant to last, don't try to keep it going artificially.
- Thank God for these people, for they mostly are godsends.
- Treasure the lessons learned; keep the good, let go of the bad.

When Hennie was a Regent University student upon our arrival in the United States, the small church we attended became our family. Jerry and Annie Horner introduced us to this church, and there we found love, support, and unbelievable care while Hennie was going through the trauma. Pastor Jim and Judy Kilpatrick became part of our daily lives during that time, but our connection sadly ended when we went back to South Africa. Though they are no longer in our lives, they are forever in our hearts. We have no doubt about the significance of our relationship, and we can't imagine going through all of that pain without them. In our hearts, our attending that church was truly a setup by God.

Other friendships that once had prime influence in our lives ended very painfully, though we know that some of them were in our lives for very specific reasons, as we were in theirs. Some of these relationships should never have ended, and we wish they never had, but for reasons beyond our control, they are now in our past. We all lost wonderful connections. Somehow we were unsuccessful to change the outcome. We chose to give the pain to God and to hold on to the good they brought to our lives, remembering how we've grown in the whole process. School fees for life lessons frequently come at staggering costs—sometimes in money, other times in tears.

We all have had friendships that were never meant to last, but rather to be used by God to shape, grow, and prepare us for the future. Those are the tough ones that cause pain and guilt to linger beyond its time. Pain was involved, yet God used it for a specific reason. We let go of the disappointment and questions, knowing that the experience made us stronger for the race ahead.

For-a-Season People

▶ They come into your life to share for a season—before they have to go.

▶ Good relationships often come with shared positive experiences, yet no deep personal connections are formed.

▶ There may be great potential for enjoyable lasting relationships that somehow never happened.

▶ Circumstances put distance between them and you. They may relocate, get married, find jobs elsewhere, or simply grow away as life seasons change.

▶ Initially you may think of them as lifelong connections, but the relationships do not survive circumstances or change.

A Healthy Response

• Cherish them for the shared experience you've had for a season.

• Treasure them as a positive memory, for they usually are uncomplicated and enjoyable.

• Let them go; neither they nor you should feel any guilt.

It was my last day at my dream job, teaching at Joubert Park Technical College in Johannesburg. I had to say good-bye. I was a young mom with changing circumstances that had called me to the next season in my life. We had our tea and cake in the staff lounge, and colleagues presented their kind remarks about our time on the same team. Then came my turn to say goodbye. I don't remember much of my speech, except my final words that resounded loudly in my soul as I was saying them: "It was good to know each one of you."

I felt hopeless in having to break those relationships. I knew they were professional ones that wouldn't survive the season change, yet I was saddened. I walked away from them as I walked away from that season. It was a marvelous season in my young life, but it had to change as my circumstances changed. None of these purely professional relationships were deep or strong enough to continue.

How many of your close friends from college or high school do you still see? Probably only a few, if any. Nothing bad happened between you; the season was simply over. You all attended different colleges, pursued different careers, and started a new season elsewhere. Many relationships survive season changes, but for the most part, they fade.

Forever People

- ▶ They are not necessarily perfect people or relationships, yet strong and loyal.
- ▶ Both sides enjoy special connections that you know will last forever.
- ▶ Commitment levels are so high that circumstances don't allow this relationship to die.
- ▶ They are very special, unusual, hard-to-find, and life-giving.
- ▶ The connection has survived challenges, changes, and even tension.
- ▶ They could be very close people, or less personal, depending on the way you relate.

A Healthy Response
- • Make sure these are healthy relationships; unhealthy ones are never *forever*.

223

- It is about commitment both ways; invest in it with patience and sacrifice.
- Become a student of the personal ones, the ones close to you, and learn how to overcome obstacles.
- If these relationships are on a professional level, protect them and stay loyal.

Only the test of time reveals the role people play in your life. Some of them are forever by choice, but somehow others you don't choose simply last. Some relationships have many reasons not to last, but they do.

I've talked about the Nusses and the Horners in earlier chapters. The Nuss family invited us for much more than dinner that first Easter we spent together. The Horners also invited us into their home, where they loved us with great humility. Both families invited us for dinner, but we stayed for life! We enjoyed countless meals, days, and holidays together; we also walked through hell with them by our sides. We live on separate coasts now, but our hearts are forever fused. They are *forever* people to us, divinely brought into our lives. No earthly force could have set this up. We will honor them forever; we are so very grateful!

Oftentimes these relationships require a fight to keep them intact. It may take effort, it may take loving people who are not perfect, and it may take going beyond what is comfortable in order to protect the purpose or goodness the friendship brings to your life. This is especially true if it's family or those in close proximity who are an integral part of your life. If you know they are God-people, i.e., ones God called you to love, ones who draw you closer to God and cause you to stretch or grow, then fight for the health of the connection. Most good things in life do not come easily; they require effort. Protecting what God intended to thrive is worth going the extra mile.

For-Never People

▶ Some kind of disappointment goes along with these connections every time because you care about them, but the connection is not meant to be.

▶ You may give mercy and walk a second mile, but to no avail.

▶ Eventually destruction and pain are inevitable.

▶ Loved ones probably warn you of the toxic nature of these connections.

▶ They instigate you to act outside your own nature, bringing out the worst in you.

▶ They may require love, but from a distance, perhaps even a great distance.

A Healthy Response

• You have no choice other than to take responsibility for allowing this negative influence in your life.

• Breaking these ties could be dangerous, so get help in ending them.

• Seek wise counsel and prepare to make life-giving decisions.

These are the relationships that need to end! They are not necessarily the ones you wish or feel the desire to terminate because they irritate you or you simply don't like them. Those are the "rather-not" people who are your teachers, who cause you to mature! The ones that need to end range from aggravating to hostile and dangerously life-threatening. You may simply have to walk away from destructive relationships that make you do things you never thought you would.

Toxic relationships with *for-never* people need to be eliminated, but you must deal with them wisely. Think it through, seek counsel, and hear from God, keeping in mind your own safety. Stop spending your time, talent, and treasure on these relationships. Whether you continue or break these connections, you will require help, because severing the relationship could leave you in pain and guilt as well as lacking forgiveness. Please talk to a trustworthy person and ask for help.

Some features of *for-never* relationships include the following: a lack of loyalty when you are not around, repeated painful events that oftentimes play out in the same way, pressure to act outside your character, uncertainty that the other person in the relationship really cares, and constant destructive incidents.

You may wonder whether you should break a relationships or not, and if so, how to break with people to whom you may be closely connected at this time. You realize they should not be in your life *forever*. They are there now, but you'd rather do life without them and definitely not have them *forever*. If this is a spouse or a family member, different rules apply. You can't just decide not to love them anymore and label them as *for-never* people! Many conditions apply in those cases, and it would be wise for you to talk to your spiritual leader or find sound counsel.

Choose Wisely

You are allowed to surround yourself with people who love you! You may choose whom to allow close to your life. You will always have challenging people with you, such as relatives, but for the most part, you have a choice. Don't have a bad attitude about the challenging ones who need to stay; you may be this very person in someone else's life! I hope not, but it's entirely possible.

You need people around you who believe in you, encourage you, and love God. On the other hand, people will disappoint you. You have to love everyone—even the obnoxious ones, yet carefully choose whom you let into your heart. Carefully choose the ones to whom you listen, the ones whose counsel you receive, and the ones you allow to play a major role in your life.

A good standard to help you make choices is the fruit in the lives of people. Without judging, decide if they resemble any part of who you want to be. No one is perfect, yet you are responsible for who you allow to speak into your life. That responsibility is especially significant when you are vulnerable, as in the midst of trials.

5. Seasons and Times

When seasons change, whether naturally, traumatically, or by choice, it does not mean God has changed. We may have to find a new standard, but in heaven everything is in order. In God's plan, nothing has been ruined for you!

After Jesus died, His disciples were baffled. The One they believed was their Savior had been crucified. They could not possibly have been more disappointed. For them everything changed, yet with God nothing changed. They gathered in secret behind locked doors, fearing for their own lives. Huddled together while reminiscing over Jesus' teachings, they must have wondered what went wrong. Did God change His mind?

While they were still talking, Jesus walked into the room. Imagine their astonishment! One minute they were afraid for their lives; the next they were in the presence of the risen Lord. They immediately knew it was, in fact, not the end of their faith but the beginning of a new and supernatural season, like they had never seen or dreamt of before.

God always, without exception, functions in perfect time and order. That fact is evident all around us. Creation happened in numbered days; the earth functions in a cycle of seasons; the sun, moon, and planets move in mathematical precision; the Jewish feasts and calendar are set according to detailed specifications. Nothing is haphazard with God. Ever!

With us, yes. On earth, certainly. With God, never!

We are tied to the effects of sin in this world, but God is not. He always operates in the fullness of time, as constantly demonstrated in the Bible. Seasons are inevitable, yet change does not mean God has changed, or that life is out of control. It means that there are things that need to be left behind in the past, and that there is a future ahead holding new beginnings and hope.

God never changes; He stays the same. He is the same in His plan, His promises, and His Person. Our lives change with seasons; nothing stays the same in our experience.

Steady Me!

We struggle in the midst of seasonal transitions, yet their success directly determines the outcome of our lives. Every season and every change presents us with choices. New faith and new vision, accompanied by new attitudes, are required of us to successfully exit one season to enter the next. In rearing kids, for example, learning curves are huge. The moment you have the one stage figured out, it's time for the next. You may even brag, proudly giving advice on how to be successful in navigating a certain stage in parenting, only to realize you are no longer there. It's time to face the next stage. If nothing else humbles you, this will! It can be either frustrating or the greatest adventure ever.

With traumatic changes, it's different, but still the same phenomenon happens. We get overwhelmed, confused, angry, and even bitter. Life can leave you sour the longer you live it, so make sure that you don't become the proverbial grumpy old person! How can we blame them? Life can leave anyone grumpy! What is easy about aging? Nothing! It's simply another season, one that will probably require more faith than you've ever needed for any other season in your life. It's the pattern of life, and it will never change this side of heaven. The only constant in the world of human beings is the fact that nothing will stay the same. Choose life, fight for peace, and listen to the right people because the outcome of transitions equals the outcome of our lives.

Help us, God, to discern the times and seasons, to hear You clearly, to grow wise in every transition, to bear the pain, and to see You while enjoying Your beauty in every circumstance.

This is good news if you are in a season of pain, for it shall pass. Seasons bring new hope, new dreams and new possibilities. It's much like day and night, where each new morning brings new mercy and a new chance to start fresh. The hard seasons will pass; the new ones will offer new beginnings. When you are in pain, it is difficult to see beyond your present circumstances. There is a new season just beyond the horizon of your own perspective. For that reason you need to keep your focus on God, for He is not trapped in your narrow-sighted view.

A Friend

The changing seasons of life are also the reason we need God-fearing people of faith in our lives. At times when we cannot manage to even glance a day ahead, we can look to a friend and believe in what that friend can see. A mere spoken word can bring renewed assurance to us, as seen in Proverbs 25:11, which says, *"A word fitly spoken is like apples of gold in settings of silver."* I don't fully understand what that statement means, but I know that's what I want from a friend when I'm hurting. How beautiful!

A friend will remind you of the words of your song when you stop singing. Season changes will do that. You may be so busy that you forget to sing. Always remember that the world needs to hear your song!

Watch Out for the Trap!

What are our options when we are in the midst of a season without vision, waning in hope, and experiencing unbearable pain?

Trauma so easily traps us into thinking it is going to last forever—

that life is over. The truth is, though, that it shall pass. Every season comes to an end. It may not be the desired ending, but that is only detrimental if you believe our earth experience is all there is to life. This life is a vapor, a door to eternity, so take heart, there is always more to life than what the eye can see.

Ride It Out

Every season or transition, no matter how painful or subtle it may be, offers options: you can either ride it out or resist the reality.

Have you ever noticed that a surfboard has no maneuverable rudder? Underneath the board are rushing waves tossed by forceful currents, while standing on the board is the surfer, who navigates the ride to stay on top of it all. His position on the waves constantly changes; he has no option to stay in place. The surfer uses the forces in play to move where he wants to go—all this while enjoying the ride!

Even when it's not for the sake of fun, the same scenario works. When we find ourselves carried about by undercurrents or powerful waves that want to take us down or to places we don't want to go, we need to stand up strong, navigate the forces, and ride them out. The more we kick and scream on that surfboard, the more treacherously dangerous our world gets.

I once witnessed a novice surfer on the waves, who was with family and friends teaching her the rudiments of surfing. While she was sitting on her board, she almost immediately drifted away into the distance. It was quite a show to watch as it transpired.

She had two major problems to address:

1) She had no idea how to surf.
2) She was sitting down passively, silently drifting away. She could at least have tried using her arms to row.

This novice had a major asset in her friends. They went after her once they realized she was being helplessly pulled into the deep far away from them. May God help us learn how to navigate the waves, stay on top of the board, and be surrounded by those who will save us in our need.

Resist the Reality

Instead of riding it out, we can resist the reality of our season. The reality in the heavenlies is that we have been saved from the dark powers in this world, but we have to face our immediate reality that requires action on our part. Ours is not a lack of faith, but faith is ineffective if unaccompanied by action.

When transitions come, seasons change, new realities set in, and we have the option to resist and harden our hearts. I witnessed an illustration of this situation many years ago on an early morning jog in my neighborhood. The promise of spring was in the air that beginning of March in Virginia. A new season was soon to rid us of all the cold, snowy weather. Christmas was long past, but this one house was still fully decorated in all the trimmings of the season. The sight stunned me momentarily. *How odd!* The decorations were seriously out of season, oddly out of place and evidence of someone who didn't care. *Someone please help those people* was my thought. They were stuck in the past! Even worse, they were missing out on what was new, what was fresh, what was exciting.

Those are also my thoughts when I see people wearing their high school styles in their late thirties. Indulge me for a second…let's give grace, but even into the late forties? Why do they do that? A year or ten is one thing, but wearing clothes from decades ago? Is it because of the cost of clothing? Maybe they feel comfortable with what they are used to wearing? Are they trying to preserve the memories of a season they loved too much to leave behind? Maybe all of the above, but my guess is that all of us get stuck at times where we had the most fun or deepest pain. Either way, to get the most out of life the way God intended, we need to learn not to resist the changing seasons but to embrace them to find their full benefit and enjoy them.

After searching high and low for meaning in life, Solomon, who was wiser than any man who had ever lived, said to eat, drink, rejoice and enjoy the fruit of your labor—it is a gift from God! Let's move on, change the mood, and get rid of Christmas in March. Go shopping or something!

The Balance

Somewhere between the savvy surfer and the passive learner is a beautiful balance when dealing with the different seasons. All of us have different ways to deal with different seasons, so we should give each other grace when seasons change. Some people find it exciting, while others who are slow movers don't appreciate changing things themselves or others who are moving. When we resist change and fail to move on, we miss out. We may have to face disappointment as we look back and realize that we missed spring, since we lingered in winter.

While You Wait

Sometimes seasons last longer than you feel able or want to wait. Be ready to accept, adapt, and abide. This is a good time to seek the company of elders—those who have been in the trenches where you now are. They have much wisdom to share, so connect with people who are not your age. God placed us in families, which is the natural structure of community. When we mingle only with others our age and befriend those who are as similar to us as possible, we miss out on the plan of God.

God loves diversity. Just look at who your family members are! Let's not ship off the elderly, but keep them in the circle of life experiences. Ask them your questions to find out how they got through the seasons they had to navigate. They have a storehouse of treasures from which to provide you with rich input that may save you years, as well as tears.

Are you tired of waiting? Ponder this Scripture:

Then the LORD answered me and said: "Write the vision and make it plain on tablets, that he may run who reads it. For the vision is yet for an appointed time. But at the end it will speak, and it will not lie. Though it tarries, wait for it; because it will surely come, it will not tarry." (Habakkuk 2:2-3)

Final Words

I've given you a plethora of words in this book, but more than words, I have shared my hope. I gave you a piece of my heart. By sharing my brokenness with you, my earnest desire is that you'll hold on to it while your own heart is being healed. May you find hope when you see how broken a life can be in one season and how wonderful life can be the next. A glimmer of hope, a breath of faith, or a glimpse of life on the other side of the river has the power to revive a broken heart just enough not to give up. Don't ever give up. It's always too soon to give up! God is alive, and you have one breath left, so dare to dream of a day when you'll wake up to the most beautiful season of your life! Your best is yet to come. With God, the best is always yet to come.

Currently, Hennie and I savor a season that used to be only a dream. We've been traveling for many months across this stunning country while experiencing nature, enjoying the people, and falling deeper in love with each other. Yes, after so many years of navigating life, rearing kids, and making ends meet, it is possible to gain a deeper connection with the love of your life. Ours was a risky step, since it is entirely possible to get to this point in life only to realize you have drifted apart and lost the priority of making love work in marriage. As I said, ours has been a dream that we were never sure would materialize, but it has. After over thirty years in ministry, we were at a significant crossroads with our last assignment completed, when we miraculously found ourselves in a season of restoration, peace, and closeness. Just the two of us, a motorhome, and the open road! This is where I was able, for the first time in thirty years, to focus on completing the writing of this book. A dream come true—a dream that has died many deaths over many years. I've prayed for you, shared with you, faced my fears, all while believing as I submit to God's season, that He will perfect those things that concern you. I was able to talk to you from all over the country as we traveled—from camping next to rushing rivers in the shadows of magnificent rock formations to being stuck in dusty little towns, hiding from gale-force winds; from sleeping amid the grandeur of giant sequoia forests to waking up several yards away from crashing waves on the Pacific Ocean; and from exploring the breathtaking Florida Keys sugar beaches with out-of-this-world sunsets to reminiscing about our family vacations in the shadows of the mysterious Blue Ridge Mountains. We traveled through mountains and meadows, farmlands and deserts; we saw where you live. We stopped in inner cities and one-horse towns. (Yes, they still exist.) We stayed overnight in shady trailer parks and elaborate RV resorts. We slept in rest stops, and we even spent time in Walmart parking lots for Wi-Fi before buying our own MiFi. Ours has been the experience of a lifetime.

God knows I'm way too hyper and easily distracted to focus this hard, so here I was in a 34-foot bus, with no job, no kids, no grandbabies, and no people I knew. There was only God and the one I love— the one whose story I was committing to paper. It was time. Initially, it was a matter of submitting to my husband, joining him on his great traveling adventure, but it ended up being as much about me as it was about him. Oh, the reward of submission! God reached deep into my heart with waves of healing, restoring my soul while brilliantly setting me up for the next season of our lives.

The greatest honor of my life has been having this opportunity to pen our story, telling about the goodness of God in our lives. I still have volumes to write, so it's in pure self-control that I have to leave you for now by concluding this assignment. Dear reader, I love you with a love that only God knows goes so deep. I feel your pain to a point of helplessness, as I know your challenges are probably deeper than I can even begin to imagine.

Let me be the voice in your desert of unfulfilled expectations in life. May I assure you that there is hope, life, and a better day ahead. You have to hold on, be faithful to your season and calling for now. Soon you'll see the day that you've only dreamed of, accompanied by the grace to cover those things that will only be perfected in eternity.

Grab the day, trust God in all things, dream the impossible, stay faithful to your spot, take a deep breath, and get up one more time. You may have been burned by life in many ways, but you also are unbroken! You carry wounds, you have accumulated scars, you face tough days, but on the inside—there where it really matters, where God reaches in and heals—you are unbroken.

Peace, grace and favor to you and yours!

Now glory be to God, who by his mighty power at work within us is able to do far more than we would ever dare to ask or even dream of—infinitely beyond our highest prayers, desires, thoughts, or hopes. May he be given glory forever and ever through endless ages because of his master plan of salvation for the Church through Jesus Christ. (Ephesians 3:20-21 TLB)

Acknowledgments

To MY FIRST LOVE, God Almighty, the One who is my all in all, I thank You for all You have done. You have called me to love, sustained me in serving, spoken to me in the dark, and soothed my aching pain. There is no greater good. There is no greater love.

This book represents a joint effort of Hennie's and mine. Without his support, our story would never have been told. Thank you, my love, for believing in me far beyond my own capabilities. You drove me around from coast to coast for a whole year to the most breathtaking places in this country, parked our motorhome, and left me to write. I missed some great hikes but appreciated every moment I had alone with God and my words. Once the manuscript was done, little did we know it was not done at all, but you never gave up!

Many have asked why Hennie did not write the book or whether he will in the future. He has no intention of ever revisiting his past pain. Maybe he will write about something fun like how to make marriage work, how to stay safe as a couple when storms hit, or why not write about RVing for a year? Believe me, it is a very spiritual exercise and highly recommended—running around the country in a motorhome with the one you love! Most of all, thank you for fighting to stay alive when no one thought it was possible.

God gave me incredible kids. Yolandie, Niel and Heinz, thank you for blindly supporting my dreams with such great honor—especially since you have a mother who can have a hundred ideas in one minute—you simply love me in and through it all. I get to be your mom, how is that even fair? I am forever honored. Matt, my son-in-law and gift from heaven, with my grandsons, Wyatt, Wesley and Walter, gave me all the more motivation to pen the goodness of God for future God-fearing generations. You are immigrant kids with the power of heaven on your side; what more do you need to bring the splendor of God to your world? You've got this!

Dr. Jerry Horner and Annie are a key part of our testimony. Our families spent fun times together and attended the same church at the time of the accident—when he was also the Dean of Biblical Studies at Regent University. Their pure, godly hearts not only touched our lives, but also that of thousands of his students all over the world. Amongst his endless accomplishments is being the editor of the New Testament of the first edition of the Spirit Filled Life Bible, undoubtedly he is one of the great theologians of our time. To us, he is the embodiment of a modern-day saint and true friend. The Horners showed us what the church should look like by their lives. He edited this manuscript in the midst of a busy schedule while still ministering in many parts of the world. Thank you.

Dr. Donald Nuss and Tessa are lifelong friends who left deep imprints of love and loyalty on our family. He edited the manuscript for medical correctness as a medical professional and as someone who witnessed it all. As a world-renowned medical pioneer, he is a brilliant scientist who, at the same time, never lost his love for people and genuine care for each of his patients. To be admired most is his deep love for God with an unwavering faith in His miraculous power. If ever I needed a surgeon, he undoubtedly would have been my first choice, but since he is a pediatric surgeon, that was never going to happen! Knowing them changed our lives for the better. Thank you.

Sandi Simonson is my Esther; she became part of my life for such a time as this. God used her to make a way for my writings to see the light of day. She convinced me I had something to say as long as it was God-breathed and offered her support, skill and sensitivity to the

ACKNOWLEDGMENTS

———

Spirit of God to iron out the wrinkles my Afrikaans left in my English writing. Without her godly and motherly support, hundreds of thousands of words would still be trapped in my heart; this assignment would forever have been too vast to me. Thank you.

My deep appreciation also goes to all of my friends who over the years believed in my ministry and counsel. In ministering and teaching you, I was the one who was ministered to and learned the most. Some of you are still young and vibrantly living out your ministry, while others will never read this book as they are, or are soon to be, with Jesus. I think of Willie Taljaard, Arlene Stallings, and Mickey McCormic who relentlessly loved and encouraged us. Thank you to all who gave us room to grow.

Thank you, Linda Stubblefield, my godsent writing specialist, who did the final editing and preparations for publishing.

Please visit us on our website for
more pictures, blogs, and
encouragement.

www.unbrokenliving.com